A Rose O' Plymouth-Town

Beulah Marie Dix

A Rose o' Plymouth-Town

A Romantic Comedy in Four Acts
by Beulah Marie Dix
and Evelyn Greenleaf Sutherland

1903
THE FORTUNE PRESS
BOSTON

DRAMATIS PERSONÆ

MILES STANDISH, Captain of Plymouth

GARRETT FOSTER, of Weston's men

JOHN MARGESON,
PHILIPPE DE LA NOYE, } of the Plymouth colonists

MIRIAM CHILLINGSLEY, cousin to the Captain

BARBARA STANDISH, wife to the Captain

RESOLUTE STORY, aunt to the Captain

ROSE DE LA NOYE .

PLACE: Plymouth in New England
PERIOD: 1622–1623

ACT I.   An early Morning in August
ACT II.   An Afternoon in October
ACT III. A Night in March
ACT IV.   The next Afternoon

Act I   Stolen Fruit

ACT I

Scene:—THE KITCHEN OF CAPTAIN STAN-DISH'S HOUSE. A rude, early-colonial interior, with a great fireplace at L. At R3 a flight of stairs goes up to the garret chambers. Door R1 to inner rooms. At C the entrance door. Latticed windows LC and L3. A cupboard with dishes and household utensils beneath the stairs at R. A great settle before the fireplace. A rude table at R. A heavy old chair or two, and some stools about the room.

When the curtain rises the lattices are swung wide and the door C is open, giving a view of Plymouth harbor and the Manomet headlands, dim and gray in the early dawn. As the act goes on, the gray light changes to rosy dawn-light, which brightens to sunlight at the entrance of Rose de la Noye.

Before the curtain rises there is distinctly heard a murmur of men's voices, a sharp, military-sounding order or two, the clash of armor, and the retreating of heavy, marching feet.

At rise of curtain, Barbara Standish, a comely young matron, is looking out at the door C. To her enter R3 Miriam Chillingsley, a slender young Puritan maid, dressed hastily, as if newly risen, and with a nightcap tied under her chin.

MIRIAM — Mistress Standish! (*runs down stairs*) Oh, Mistress Standish!

BARBARA — Why, child, what called you from your bed so early?

> *Enter R1 Aunt Resolute Story, a plump old gentlewoman, in a short bed-gown, worn over an elaborately quilted petticoat, and a frilled nightcap.*

AUNT RESOLUTE — Called her from bed? 'Tis enough to call any poor body from their last bed of all—this growling o' men, and clash o' breast-plates, and trampling as of Bashan bulls—and the sun not over the sea-edge! Truly, one should have nerves of bow-string, ere one come to so nerve-racking a corner! What's toward?   *Sits on settle*

MIRIAM — Ay, what is it hath happened? I heard men speak, and Rose—she hath run away and left me —she's nowhere in the room.

BARBARA — 'Tis no cause for fear. The Captain was summoned in haste, and as we were already well roused up, our wild Rose was loath to creep back to bed on so fair a morning. She hath run to the spring—

AUNT RESOLUTE — The Captain summoned? What is amiss? Who hath done wrong?

BARBARA — Nay, whence begins all the wrong in our little colony in these days? *She begins to set the room to rights, straightening chairs, wiping and arranging dishes in cupboard, etc.*

MIRIAM — 'Tis again those lusty men of Master Weston's—they who are staying with us till they plant their settlement at Wessagusett?

BARBARA—Ay, another brawl in the quarters of Master Weston's men, and the Captain called forth in haste to cool their hot bloods.

MIRIAM—Those wicked firebrands! I heard John Margeson say they were naught but the off-scourings of London's streets and prisons.

AUNT RESOLUTE—John Margeson! Ay, a worthy citizen he of our new, merry commonwealth of Plymouth! A merry commonwealth, good lack! A blockhouse, psalms a plenty, and now and then a bear!

BARBARA—Nay, sure, dear Aunt, our little Plymouth, far though it be, is a sweet and quiet spot.

AUNT RESOLUTE—Quiet? Quiet? Good lack, so is the grave quiet! An you be so fain to be quiet, why not go further than Plymouth, to the one place quieter than Plymouth?   *Points upward*

BARBARA—Pray you, Aunt, an you hold our poor Plymouth so in contempt, why came you hither from your gay London town?

AUNT RESOLUTE—When a female hath lived to over-ripe years, she cometh to know all the gay thrills that even gay London town can give her. I came to your little Plymouth in the hope that I might find in the wilderness one last new sensation; and for a new sensation I would go to—*Rises excitedly, points downward*

BARBARA—(*warningly*) Aunt!

AUNT RESOLUTE—Lord, why shouldn't I say the word? One hears it oft enough in your endless Plymouth sermons.   *Sits*

MIRIAM—And hast thou found thy new sensation, Mistress Story?

AUNT RESOLUTE—What sensation hath your Plymouth to offer, unless sensation grow in a cornfield? I go out; I hear the men talk of how the corn is growing in the fields. I come in; I hear the women talk of how the corn is boiling in their kettles. Oh, rich sensations has this, your Plymouth.

MIRIAM—Nay, Aunt Resolute.

AUNT RESOLUTE—Oh, a paradise is Plymouth to you, little Miriam, since it doth nest that rare bird, John Margeson.

MIRIAM—Nay, Mistress Story, to speak so of an excellent—

AUNT RESOLUTE—Excellent? Ay, that's the plague of it, that so excellent a man should be so sad a weakling. The like of him to speak ill of Weston's men! Knaves Weston's men may be, but, God wot, they have blood in them, ay, red blood, with a jump to it! Your excellent Margeson—verily, I think his blood is green!

MIRIAM—O, Mistress Standish, she would rate Master Weston's knaves above John Margeson—those rogues of Wessagusett men!

BARBARA—Nay, nay, dear lass, there may be good men in Master Weston's company.

MIRIAM—You may speak forbearingly of them, Mistress Standish. And yet you are waiting here now, I know, in very fear lest they do harm unto the Captain, your husband.

BARBARA—Nay, I have no fear for Captain Standish, my husband, though the whole three score of Weston's bullies were pitted against him.

AUNT RESOLUTE—Ay, my nephew, the Captain, hath his faults, but he's no John Margeson to be frightened by the bleat of a ewe—no, nor by the horns of a ram, neither!   *Goes up to door C*

MIRIAM—(*in tears*) I scarce wake when I'm chidden!

BARBARA—Nay, but we meant not to chide you, dear. (*Rose is heard laughing outside*)   Hark!   Yonder comes our Rose to sweeten our humor.   Dry thine eyes.

MIRIAM—Yea, 'tis Rose indeed. (*runs to door C*) And with her comes—

AUNT RESOLUTE — Your John Margeson, mistress. The ewes must lie safe in fold since he's abroad.

MIRIAM—Ay, 'tis John.

AUNT RESOLUTE—Thou art scarce apparelled for a levee.   Thy nightcap—

MIRIAM—(*snatching off cap*) Good lack, I had forgot! (*runs up stairs*) But you—you also—look but at your cap!
    Exit Miriam R3.

AUNT RESOLUTE—Nay, when a female hath lived to my years, it matters little if she go abroad nightcapped —or bide at home wi' nightcap and naught else! Rest you fair, niece Barbara, rest you fair!
    Exit Aunt Resolute R1.

BARBARA—Come your ways in, Rose!   Truly, you bring the sweet o' the morning with you!

Enter C Rose de la Noye, a little, curly-haired lass of seventeen, dressed after the Puritan fashion, but herself without a trace of the Puritan in face or bearing. She carries a red rose in her hand, and comes running in, laughing.

Behind her come Philippe de la Noye, a dark, sturdy Huguenot lad of eighteen, and John Margeson, a young man in his early twenties, heavy and rather sullen-faced. The two lads carry between them a bucket of water.

Rose—Good greeting to you, Mistress Barbara. I go forth unattended; I return—regard! (*points to the lads who have paused in doorway*) Set down the bucket yonder, good servants, and I will prepare the breakfast. Come, Mistress Standish, what will you? A boiled capon, a roasted neat's tongue, a pasty of venison, an olave pie, a roasted swan—or a ravishing porridge of beans? Ah, I know ere I ask. 'Twill be the divine, the ecstatic bean porridge! With it I have lived, and with it I shall die—and of it I shall die, if I bide out my life in this lost corner of the world! Why stand you twain idle there? Pray you now, John Margeson, fill me the kettle, and you, Brother Philippe, mend me the fire.

John—Suffer me do it. *John and Philippe mend fire, fill kettle, etc.*

Rose—Now do you go in, mistress, and leave me, for to cook bean porridge doth require a skill, a delicacy, the fine hand—you Englishwomen have not the art!

Barbara—But little shrew, may I not cook in mine own kitchen?

Rose—What have you, the mistress of this castle, to do with cooking? Also, you are no cook! Go in and put on a cambric kerchief, and so be beautiful to our eyes.

Barbara—Hush, hush! You giddy-tongued flatterer!

Rose—You call me ill names, and I will no longer adorn your house with my presence. Go, leave me to work! *Morbleu*, will you—

Philippe—Rose! Rose!   *Crosses to her*

Rose—Ay, see how she will drive me to swear! And my immortal soul, alas, my immortal soul! Go! *Par le sambleu*—

Barbara—(*covering her ears with her hands*) I'm gone! I'm gone!

     Exit Barbara R1.

Rose—*Sa, sa, p'tit, Philippe!* The naughty word was so near the lip, 'twas better to let it forth than swallow it to spoil my porridge. Also you do not understand the French tongue, eh, John Margeson?

John—Nay, mistress.

Rose—A pity! 'Tis a noble tongue, an extraordinary tongue, a tongue with possibilities! (*lays cloth on table R, with Philippe's help*) And now since you two have been drawers of water, be also my hewers of wood. You will fetch it me, will you not, Philippe, honey?

Philippe—Ay, surely, sister. I'll fetch an armful of wood for you, and John shall bring one for sweetheart Miriam.

John—Whose sweetheart?

PHILIPPE—Why, yours.

JOHN—Who saith so?

PHILIPPE—All the town.

JOHN—Believe not all the town says.   *Starts to door C*

    Re-enter Miriam R3.

MIRIAM—Good morrow to you all. Good morrow, John.   *Comes down stairs*

JOHN—(*indifferently*) Good morrow, good morrow, Miriam.   Is it wood you bid me fetch, Rose?

ROSE—Ay.

MIRIAM—John, a moment.   John, cannot you—I had—I wished—

JOHN—Time presses, Miriam.   What is it you would say?

MIRIAM—Sure, I've near forgot.   You spoke so sharp, you put it from my mind.

JOHN—Perhaps you will recall it ere we meet again.

MIRIAM—(*eagerly*) When shall that be?

JOHN—I know not.   I must sail this morning for Nauset with the Captain.

MIRIAM—To Nauset?   So far a journey, John?

JOHN—Why, what matters it?

MIRIAM—What matters it!

JOHN—Yea, I know not how I have deserved so large a place in your thoughts that it should matter. (*to Rose*) God be wi' you!

    Exit John C.

MIRIAM—John! *Leans against door-frame, back to room*

ROSE—Pig that he is! Why dost thou not kill him, Philippe?

PHILIPPE—What quarrel have I with friend John?

ROSE—Oh, you men, you men! You will uphold each other in all knavery!

PHILIPPE—But Rose, if John doth not love Miriam—

ROSE—But Philippe, if Miriam loves John!

PHILIPPE—Yet still 'tis no crime though he—

ROSE—No crime? No crime? 'Tis a hanging crime if a lad with red blood in him doth meet love in a sweet maid's eyes and not look loving back—when it is summer-time, when—Ay, but what can a lad such as thou know of these matters?

PHILIPPE—(*indignantly*) Eh?   *Miriam sobs aloud*

ROSE—My poor Miriam! Listen, Philippe, 'tis you must be vastly gentle to her.

PHILIPPE—(*huffily*) Nay, I know naught of such matters.

ROSE—She is as my own sister, I say. Be you as her own brother, and kind to her as a brother.

PHILIPPE—Methinks, Rose, the kindness here must come from you.

ROSE—How kinder than I am always to her?

PHILIPPE—By being more unkind to John Margeson. (*goes to door C; speaks hesitatingly to Miriam*) May I pass hence, mistress?

MIRIAM—Oh! (*moves from door-way*) Forgive me!

PHILIPPE—Mayhap you'd not be loath to walk forth a pace or two? 'Tis a fair morning. Belike you'll feel freer out o' doors. There's the fresh breeze and sweet smelling things.

MIRIAM—(*indifferently*) Yea, I'll come.

Exeunt Philippe and Miriam C.

ROSE—By being unkind to John Margeson! What mean he? Why, can he dare— Oh, oh! Find me two men, and I'll find you a fool and a half! Nay, I wrong men; I'll find you two fools! Slight my Miriam that loves him for—

Re-enter John C, with armful of wood

Now to see! (*without looking round*) Oh, are you come, dear?

JOHN—Dear!   *Lets wood fall to floor*

ROSE—'Tis you? Methought it was my brother Philippe. Oh, pardon me that I—that I—

JOHN—What is it I have to pardon that you called me by a name so pleasant to hear?

ROSE—I thought it might be that you would take amiss—

JOHN—(*ardently*) How could I take it amiss?

ROSE—Then you're not angry?

JOHN—Angry!

ROSE—(*laughing*) Then pray you, pick up my wood for me, good John. *Sets table with plates, cups, a loaf, etc.*

JOHN—Ay, Rose.   *Places wood by hearth*

ROSE—John. Methinks the name comes sweetly to my lips.

JOHN—Rose! Can you feel that? My name?

ROSE—There was a time I had an attachment, an honest tenderness for one that bore the name of John. Some ways you do recall him to me.

JOHN—(*jealously*) A lover, was it?

ROSE—You might call it so, if to love truly make a lover. Brown eyes he had, dear eyes, and he would lick my hand so tenderly—

JOHN—Lick? A lover? What do you talk of, Rose?

ROSE—Why, of my well-beloved dog, English John, we called him. He's dead now two years, poor sweetheart!

JOHN—A cur dog!

ROSE—Nay, there be dogs that none may call cur, as there be men one may call naught else! Oh, oh! You're angry in earnest now!

JOHN—Do you think it kindly, mistress, to play thus with a friendly heart?

ROSE—Do you think it manly, John Margeson, to play with a loving heart?

JOHN—I know not what you mean.

ROSE—You will not know. It is of Miriam we speak. And you do know. Speak truly.

JOHN—Do you hold it Christian charity to condemn a man for that the gossips have mauled him with their idle tongues? It is naught but gossip, I tell you. I have never spoken what may be construed love to any maid in the colony or plighted faith to any.

ROSE—And since you have not sealed a formal betrothal, you do hold yourself free? May one not speak without words, and stand bound thereby? Do you hold yourself free, I say?

JOHN—Would you judge otherwise?

ROSE—Nay, I'll take instruction in this case from you.

JOHN—Will you take instruction from me in aught else, beside, sweet Rose?

ROSE—Perchance 'tis in me to give you some excellent instruction myself, sir.

JOHN—And I may come hither to receive it, then?

ROSE—Surely, I have no right to shut the door on Captain Standish's friends.

JOHN—I thank you.

ROSE—In the end you will not thank me, more than the lad thanks the rod.

JOHN—I'll lay the warning to heart, be sure!

Exit John C, laughing.

ROSE—You will? (*runs to door*) I warned him fairly! So he will come seeking me and leave my Miriam to weep? Oh, I'll punish you—I'll punish you roundly! Hey, John Margeson, I'll lead you such a dance! You'll ache for't!

An armful of green corn flies through window L, and after it enter headlong Garrett Foster, a well-favored young dare-devil of twenty, coatless and bareheaded.

ROSE—Oh!

GARRETT—Hide me! Hide me quick!

ROSE—You've been stealing corn!

GARRETT—Most evidently! And also, if they take me, I'll be flogged. Where can I hide?

ROSE—I'm not helping you! I won't help you, I say!

GARRETT—(*catching her by the wrist*) Mistress, did you ever see a man flogged?

ROSE—No, nor want to see one.

GARRETT—Then you'd best hide me quick. 'Tis hardly prettier to see than to feel. *Dashes to door RI*

ROSE—No, no! Mistress Standish is within! Stop there!

GARRETT—(*hiding by cupboard, in angle of stairs*) They're coming. Don't tell!

ROSE—But I—but I—

GARRETT—Don't tell, I say!

Re-enter John C, hastily.

JOHN—Rose! Rose! Have you seen—

ROSE—O John! I'm so frightened! ·A man jumped in at our window but now, and—and—

JOHN—Which way did he run? Beggarly thief! The Captain will flay him alive for this.

Rose—Flay! Oh! He—he jumped in at the window, and—and he ran out again by the door! Did you not see? Run, run, John! Stop him! That way, I pray you, run!

John—The thief! You do well to wish him caught!

Exit John C, running.

Rose—Run, run, good John! That way! Yea, but I wish you may catch him!

Garrett—(*coming forward*) I am your very slave for this, mistress—Mistress Rose. (*Rose stands back to, at window, ignoring his presence*) I offered you my humble thanks, mistress. I am in your debt. I pray you believe—(*strikes his fist on table*) Zounds, mistress, are you dumb?

Rose—(*turning*) Are you deaf? Did you not hear me swear but now you were halfway to the shore? Verily, you cannot be in two places at once, nor will I be forsworn.

Garrett—Oh, but there's been ample time for me to have dodged that thick-skull, made a circuit through Dr. Fuller's dooryard, and returned hither again.

Rose—And pray, who bade you return?

Garrett—If I waited to be bidden, I had often stood on the wrong side of men's doors.

Rose—You stand far on the wrong side of our door now. Pack hence!

Garrett—(*sits by table*) Wherefore?

Rose—Lest along with our corn you carry away our kettle to cook it in, and our spoons and trenchers to eat it withal.

Garrett—Nay, so I have the corn, I can shift with my fingers.

Rose—Are you so hungry, then? Truly, you have not the air of it.

Garrett—I'll not claim I'm starving. But if you had kept life alive these weary weeks on salt ship's beef and biscuits swarming with—

Rose—Come! These are not pretty stories. And so the corn waved—

Garrett—Ay, the corn beckoned with fair green fingers and said—Taste an I be not sweet!

Rose—And the corn whispered not—I am thy neighbor's corn?

Garrett—You know the wise saw?

Rose—Nay.

Garrett—As to stolen fruit and its sweetness?

Rose—Stolen fruit—

Garrett—And truly the biscuits swarmed with—

Rose—Hush, hush! (*cuts slice from loaf*) Eat of this, and forget the biscuits. 'Tis of my cooking, so you must find it good.

Garrett—Nay, I have no will to beg food of you.

Rose—Tut, tut! You that have such proud stomachs deserve to have empty stomachs. There! (*breaks a piece from slice of bread, nibbles at it*) I'll bid you eat with me.   Will that salve your honor?

GARRETT—I thank you, mistress. (*takes bread and eats*) And on mine honor, had I had such inviting to my lively biscuits, I had found them ambrosia.

ROSE—Dear, dear!   The civil thief!   *Curtsies*

GARRETT—And the uncivil hostess to cry thief!

ROSE—But you are no guest of my choosing.

GARRETT—Faith, I'd not be here, though, were it not for you.   'Twas right kind of you to aid me.

ROSE—Aid you?   Nay, flatter not yourself.   I wished to see good John Margeson run with his long legs. He's stoutening fast; 'tis excellent that he run.   And what a stitch he will have in his side, poor John!

GARRETT—(*laying hand on the knife in his belt*) An he laid hands on me, he had had something sharper than that in his side.

ROSE—Verily, we are a great fire-eater—now that John hath run round the corner!

GARRETT—(*rising*) 'Sdeath!   Do you think that I—

ROSE—Turn all your anger to the bread, I pray you. Another slice?

GARRETT—Ay.

ROSE—You are one of Weston's men, I take it?   Their ways and manners are known to us, you see.

GARRETT—I'm bound to plant at Wessagusett, yes.

ROSE—And what do you think to do there?

GARRETT—Grow tobacco.

ROSE—What!

GARRETT—Why not? They grow it in Virginia.

ROSE—But this is not Virginia!

GARRETT—'Tis all in America. What difference?

ROSE—You'll find a difference when winter comes. You'll not roam about without your doublet then.

GARRETT—Faith, but I think I will. For I have no doublet.

ROSE—Now who was it was so crack-brained as to send the like of you to settle for yourself in a new country?

GARRETT—My kinsfolk sent me. What would you? A younger son, with no inheritance! My uncle, Garrett Foster, he for whom I am named, he supplied me with bare necessaries, and bade me never come trouble him again. And I gambled away the bare necessaries when we put in at Plymouth in Devonshire. And here I am, bare indeed!

ROSE—Tut, tut! And you are to plant a colony! Will you eat another slice of bread?

GARRETT—Nay, I could not eat another mouthful, not even of ambrosia. 'Twas good bread, though.

ROSE—Surely! Did I not say I made it? I can cook better, spin faster, and dance longer than any maid in New Plymouth.

GARRETT—Dance? You are no kin to the Puritan captain, I'll wager!

Rose—Captain Standish is no Puritan, and he hath danced in his day.   But true enough, I am no kin to him.   I am only gracious to live in his house because I love Mistress Standish and their cousin Miriam. 'Tis a sad colony, this, Garrett Foster.   There's not much here to love.

Garrett—But you—

Rose—Oh, I came hither to keep the house for my brother Philippe, but they said for that I was not old and wrinkled, I was not sober enough to rule a household, and I must bide under another's household rule.

Garrett—Methinks I'd trust you over a house, now, to-day!

Rose—Oh, your obliged servant, sir!   But I'd not trust you in the cornfield that lay beside my house.

Garrett—I would you did not taunt me with that.

Rose—Have you not deserved it?

Garrett—No!   On my soul, no!   What grows out of doors, is't not for any man?

Rose—Not when another hath had sore trouble to make it grow.   Why, corn is as gold in this bleak new world of ours.

Garrett—I'll grant you're right, and 'twas a rascally prank.   But for one prank, do I lose the right of a gentleman?   *Tries to take her hand*

Rose—When you come into our cottage by its door, like a gentleman, I'll think of treating you as one.

Garrett—Why, nothing easier! (*steps out at door C,*

comes in again) There now, I claim my privilege. A salute, as you would give it to a gentleman!

ROSE—(*dodging*) You do not play fair!

GARRETT—(*chasing her*) And you do not pay fair!

ROSE—You were best not tarry to take the stakes. Captain Standish may come.

GARRETT—Hang your Captain Standish! Do you think I fear him?

ROSE—(*at door C*) It's well you do not, sir. He's coming up the path now.

GARRETT—(*running to window*) The devil!

ROSE—His enemies think him so. Nay, you cannot go by the window. He'll see you.

GARRETT—(*running to door*) The door—

ROSE—(*barring his way*) Oh, no! How happy you do not fear him! Now what will you tell him about that corn?

GARRETT—Devil take the corn! If he see me 'twill all come out!

MIRIAM—(*without*) Rose! Rose!

GARRETT—Curse it! *Flings corn on settle, drops down between end of settle and fireplace, where the high back of the settle screens him from the sight of those in the room*

> *Re-enter Miriam C, followed by Standish, a well set-up, soldierly man of thirty-eight, in the military dress of the period, with a long cloak over his arm.*

MIRIAM—You have set all in order? Forgive my lingering, Rose. I had not guessed it so late.

STANDISH—Good morrow, Major Rose! *Rose takes the cloak from Standish, and flings it over corner of settle, hiding the corn.*

Re-enter Barbara R1.

BARBARA—You are returned, Miles? Good welcome!

STANDISH—Ay, sweetheart, returned, and none the worse except in temper, and breakfast will set that right.

BARBARA—And our kind Rose hath prepared for us already. Sit at once. *Starts to fireplace. Standish and Miriam sit at table.*

ROSE—(*intercepting Barbara*) Nay, you sit too, Mistress Standish.

BARBARA—But little Rose, you are not to serve us always. Suffer me to—

ROSE—There, there! Will you spoil good porridge by ill serving? Sit you down! Captain, command her be seated, else I'll throw the porridge fair in the fire.

BARBARA—A wilful wench must have her way! *Sits at table.*

Re-enter R1 Aunt Resolute, conventionally dressed.

AUNT RESOLUTE—Be the wars over, nephew? You're welcome back!   *Sits at table*

GARRETT—(*to Rose*) 'Tis vengeance hot here!

ROSE—(*at fireplace*) If we may believe the preachers, there be hotter corners yet for men who steal their neighbors' corn.

BARBARA—Rose! *Rose crosses and sits at table. Standish says grace in dumb-show. Rose rises, fetches kettle from fire and serves porridge.*

BARBARA—So the matter for which they called you forth still disturbs you, Miles?

STANDISH—Not the matter, but that I might not lay my hands on the workers of the matter. When I came to the quarters of those rogues of Wessagusett men, all was at sleepy peace—fair white lambs that they be! *Garrett puts out his arm, secures a stool, and settles himself more comfortably in his hiding place, observed only by Aunt Resolute.*

BARBARA—So it is with all their mischief!

STANDISH—Well, my time will come later. The first man of them I take self-convicted of breaking the colony laws—I'll make an example of him!

ROSE—And what would you do to him, Captain?

STANDISH—It depends on what the man had done, lass. Now, for instance, if I come on one of the corn thieves who are wasting our fields, I'll have him stripped and flogged through the settlement.

ROSE—Do you mean that in earnest, Captain? In earnest?

STANDISH—In sore earnest. The laws of the colony are not made for a laughing-stock.

AUNT RESOLUTE—Nay, 'tis a cruel, harsh punishment. Whipped? For a paltry ear or so of corn? Mean and cruel, say I!

STANDISH—Not cruel, when 'tis deserved. A paltry ear of corn? Every ear of corn closes death's open door in our black winters. 'Tis better one stole gold of us than corn. John Margeson says—

AUNT RESOLUTE—John Margeson!

STANDISH—Ay, he hath eyes, and his eyes saw a thief in our cornfield but an hour agone. He gave chase, but the man out-ran him. Now if I had that man—
                    The people at table talk in dumb-show

GARRETT—(*to Rose, as she crosses to fire*) Rose!

ROSE—*Tudieu!* Did you not hear him? Be quiet and sit close.

GARRETT—'Tis cursed hot! My throat is parched.

ROSE—Hush! Wait! *Takes gourd from end of fireplace*

BARBARA—Come, come, child, will you never sit and eat?

ROSE—(*fills gourd at water bucket*) A moment till I weaken the porridge, good Mistress Standish. (*gives gourd to Garrett*) There!

GARRETT—I thank you mightily.   *Drinks*

ROSE—(*sits at table*) Now you shall see. I will eat thrice as much as any for this delay.

STANDISH—Faith, you attack nobly, Major Rose. 'Tis well we are going to fetch fresh stores from Nauset; you'd exhaust our supply else.

BARBARA—To Nauset this day?

STANDISH—If the wind hold from the westward, yes.

Rose—Ay, 'tis still a western wind by the smoke. You will have to leave us so soon as you have eaten?

Standish—The self-same instant.

Rose—(*clapping her hands*) Good! Good!

Barbara—(*indignantly*) "Good," sayest thou?

Rose—O Mistress Standish! Nay, I—I but meant 'twas good to see how brave an answer he ever hath for duty.

Aunt Resolute—(*aside to Rose*) Flutter not too oft near a hidden nest. Too many hunters know the trick.

Rose—O Mistress Story! Thou knowest—

Aunt Resolute—I know that the lad hath broad shoulders and brave eyes. 'Tis not of such lads I make tales.

Rose—God bless thee!

Barbara—Come and go, we never have sight of thee, Miles.

Standish—Nay, Barbara, I— *Garrett smothers a cough*

Miriam—(*startled*) Oh!

Barbara—Why, child, what is it?

Miriam—I thought I heard—

Rose—Nay, little goose, 'tis not John Margeson you hear. Let me fill your bowl once more, Mistress Standish.

Barbara—Why, I've not yet eaten—

Rose—No matter! You want some more—I know you want some more! (*runs to fireplace; speaks aside to Garrett*) Be quiet! Lord! Lord! You must be quiet!

GARRETT—There's a draught from the window fair across my neck. Rose, I'll have to sneeze in a minute.

ROSE—Sneeze? You shall not! You shall die first!

GARRETT—I can't help it! I—can't! I—

ROSE—Quick, then! *Diable!* Quick! *Garrett sneezes violently. Rose at same time makes pantomime of sneezing*

MIRIAM—Oh, bless me!

STANDISH—Good lack, what a sneeze! 'Twas the sneeze of a horse-trooper.

AUNT RESOLUTE—Nay, 'tis naught to worry on. I have sneezed that sneeze myself when I was young— Ay, many a time!

BARBARA—Why, Rose, child, whence got you such a cold?

MIRIAM—Rose, you did not wear your thin shoes to the spring?

ROSE—Yes, yes, but 'tis no matter. A sneeze—that's naught.   *Returns to table*

BARBARA—You are so heedless, feather-pate.

STANDISH—Nay, you must not let yourself fall ill, our Rose.

ROSE—Oh, I'm not ill—not ill! (*Garrett stifles a cough*) Oh! Captain Standish, let me serve you more porridge. (*crosses to fireplace; to Garrett*) Don't you dare do that again! I'm near dead of it.

GARRETT—I'm going to. I can't help it, Rose. That cursed draught—

Rose—Well, sneeze then, and let the Captain find you, if he will!

Garrett—'Tis no use. I— *Garrett sneezes loudly and Rose pretends to sneeze.*

Miriam—O my goodness!

Standish—Why, why, Major!

Barbara—There, 'tis enough. That child must have a drink of bitter herbs.   *Goes to cupboard*

Rose—O Mistress Standish! Nay, I do not want your bitter herbs.   *Comes to table*

Barbara—Indeed, you do want them, if ever a lass did. (*prepares herbs*) And now after this remember to dress yourself fittingly ere you venture out in the damp and the dew.

Aunt Resolute—Ay, bitter herbs oft come after such sneezing. I've drunk the bitter herbs too in my time.

Rose—Did they cure thee? No?

Aunt Resolute—Nay, time did that. But bitter herbs be wholesome.

Miriam—(*rises and starts to fireplace*) Shall I fetch the hot water?

Rose—(*Seizing Miriam, with a loud shriek*) Oh! Do not thou meddle with my matters! Sit thee down, Miriam! If I must drink those bitter herbs, 'tis I who'll brew them. But oh! I hate your herb drink, Mistress Standish. I will not take it. 'Tis so bitter— 'twill make me ill indeed! (*Barbara starts to fire*) Nay, nay, trouble not yourself! I'll fetch the hot water, if

I must. (*runs to fire*) But I do not want it, I tell you, I— (*aside to Garrett*) I hear you! You'll kill us both, plague on you!

GARRETT—I'm cursed sorry! *Garrett sneezes, and Rose again makes pretense of sneezing.*

BARBARA—That settles it! Now there's no need to gainsay me further. Rose, bring the hot water. (*Rose unwillingly brings the kettle, and Barbara brews the drink*) There, it is brewing bravely. Now sit you down snugly in the chimney-corner with me, like a good lass, and drink it steaming hot. *Starts to lead Rose to settle*

ROSE—Nay, nay, Mistress Standish, I do not like to be cosseted when I am ill. Take thy hands from me, prithee!

BARBARA—Why, Rose! Sweetheart!

ROSE—O Mistress Standish, I do love thee, I do—my heart on't!—but prithee leave me alone now, leave me alone! *Sits on end of settle nearest to Garrett*

RARBARA—(*returning to table*) Miles, I do fear me our poor Rose is truly ill.

AUNT RESOLUTE—Wilt never learn that some illnesses must wear themselves out? Let the lass rest.

STANDISH—Nay, had I not best summon Dr. Fuller hither?

MIRIAM—Let me run fetch him.

BARBARA—Nay, stay a little. *Talks with Standish*

ROSE—(*raising mug to her lips*) Bah! This fearsome stuff! I abominate it! I loathe it! (*Garrett smothers a laugh*) Now mark me! 'Tis you shall drink it, Garrett Foster. 'Tis you have the cold, not I. 'Tis you did the sneezing, when truth's said.

GARRETT—Poor lass! Give it me here! (*takes a swallow*) Ugh! 'Tis fair devilish!

ROSE—'Tis I know that. Shut your eyes and drink.
Watches him, not heeding the others

STANDISH—(*rising*) Ay, I'll say a word to the Doctor, as I go down the hill.

BARBARA—You must go forth now, husband?

STANDISH—I bade the men await me at the landing. Nay, 'tis not for long. We'll return the day after to-morrow. Fret not, sweetheart. If you need a man for aught till I return, call on Philippe, remember, and so— (*takes his cloak from settle, exposing corn beneath*) What's this? Faith of a soldier, what's this?

ROSE—(*springing up*) O me! We're sped!

STANDISH—Young corn, and freshly plucked? Nay, Barbara, if we devour it now, what shall we have to keep us through the winter? How couldest thou, wife?

BARBARA—There is no one of our household plucked it, Miles. I know not how it came hither. Thou knowest we would not pluck the corn.

MIRIAM—Why, sure, 'tis witchcraft!

ROSE—Nay, nay, no witchcraft, not in the least, I do assure you. 'Twas I gathered it.

ALL—You? Rose!

ROSE—I. You know I'm not of your sober blood. The sun of France warmed mischiefs in me. 'Twas a madcap whim took me, to do a thing forbid, 'twas—

AUNT RESOLUTE—A brave fight, little Major!

BARBARA—And is that the mischief hath worried you ill, Rose? (*starts toward her*) O Rose!

ROSE—Do not come near me!

STANDISH—Faith, I could not have believed it of the lass! What set you to do such a thing? A thing so wanton, so hurtful, so—

ROSE—Oh, I—I—   *Sobs*

GARRETT—(*rises and comes forward*) Mistress Rose is generous—and mistaken. She did not pluck the corn.

AUNT RESOLUTE—And there speaks another good soldier!

STANDISH—You, is it, Garrett Foster—Foster of Weston's men? Then it's not far to look for the thief John Margeson saw. So you have been concealing this fellow and his plunder, Rose?

GARRETT—I frightened her into concealing me.

ROSE—Nay, he frightened me not. I—

STANDISH—You confess the theft then, sirrah?

GARRETT—Ay. And now what next?

STANDISH—(*motioning to door C*) Go out before me.

GARRETT—To the whipping-post? I, a gentleman?

STANDISH—To the whipping-post. Thou, a thief.

GARRETT—(*with a short laugh*) Ay, and more than thief before a man lays whip to me! *Draws his knife and holds it ready behind him.*

ROSE—Garrett Foster! What have you there behind you? Give it me. I bid you give it to me. *For a moment Garrett looks at Rose, then he lays his knife in her hand*

ROSE—(*turning to Standish*) You see. He trusts me. He is an unarmed man, and he has eaten of my bread. I'll not have him whipped—do you hear, Captain of Plymouth? He shall not suffer a thief's shame for a boy's prank—he who has eaten of my bread!

BARBARA—Miles, I beg of you, Miles! Mayhap the lad was hungry, mayhap—

STANDISH—Hungry? (*Looks at Garrett, with some amusement*) Verily, he hath a starved look!

AUNT RESOLUTE—Do none steal save from hunger? I trapped thee in my apple orchard once on a time, Captain of Plymouth!

BARBARA—In pity, Miles, do not deal too harshly—

ROSE—'Tis I will be whipped, if any's whipped. And I'll not be whipped while I've Garrett Foster's knife!
Thrusts it out toward Standish, handle foremost

STANDISH—(*laughing in spite of himself*) Thou art terrible! (*takes knife from her*) Well, Garrett Foster, your skin is saved for the present.

GARRETT—Gramercy for that, Captain! I'm long your debtor.   *Starts for door*

STANDISH—Nay, you part not so easily. Your judgment's yet to be spoke; now hear it ere you part. Sit you down, yonder on the settle. (*Garrett sits unwillingly*) Now, Mistress Rose, sit you down there! Sit you down! (*Rose sits beside Garrett*) Now, Mistress Rose, for the part you had in this roguery, you may husk and roast that pile of corn, and you, Garrett Foster, for your part, will not stir from that spot till you have eaten it—ay, every jot!

GARRETT—All of it? Lord! All of it?

STANDISH—To the last kernel.

GARRETT—I've just eaten one breakfast.

STANDISH—So much the unluckier for your stomach. That, or—   *Points to door*

GARRETT—I take it, I can eat it.

STANDISH—I take it you can.   *Turns away to door*

ROSE—Corn's no bad change from porridge—and you robbed me of my breakfast. You may count on me for an ear or twain.   *Rose and Garrett begin to husk corn*

BARBARA—I thank you that you did spare him, Miles.

STANDISH—'Tis a knave unwhipped that deserves to be. But I'd pardon a worse than he for your sake, wench.

> *Exeunt Standish and Barbara C, Miriam and Aunt Resolute R.*

ROSE—If you be not sick of the taste of roasted corn soon! Yet I have heard that stolen fruit—

GARRETT—It's true enough. Stolen fruit is—(*he takes her hand, as it rests on the edge of the settle, and suddenly kisses it*) 'Tis monstrous sweet!

CURTAIN

your stor⋯

Points ⋯

Turns away to ⋯

⋯ your sake, ⋯

⋯ the vice of roasted ⋯

⋯ swell

CURTAIN

ACT II

*Scene:—THE DOORYARD OF CAPTAIN STAN-
DISH'S COTTAGE. At L the rude porch of the cottage, with a door opening into the house. At R an old
tree stump. The tall trees, with their red or russet autumn
foliage, grow up to the edge of the dooryard. At back,
through an opening in the trees, can be seen the fields, with
the shocks of corn, the harbor, and the distant headlands.
The golden autumn light lies on all the fields and the wood-
land, and the leaves are falling softly.*

*At rise of curtain, Standish sits reading in a great chair
upon the porch. Barbara sits near by, spinning at her
wheel.*

BARBARA—(*singing*)

> Now my love is roving gone,
> Welladay, welladay!
> Which makes me sigh and moan,
> Evermore still!

STANDISH—Barbara! (*after a moment*) Barbara!

BARBARA—What is it, Miles?

STANDISH—Hath Garrett Foster fetched in those pumpkins?

BARBARA—Pumpkins, Miles? What hast thou to do therewith? Verily, I thought thee leagues hence with thy famous Julius Cæsar.

STANDISH—May I not have a respect for the great Roman, and yet have a weakness for pumpkin sauce?

BARBARA—For your comfort then—the pumpkins are safely housed! (*sings*)

> Now must I weep in woe,
> Now must I mourning go,
> No comfort will I know,
> Since my dear's away!

Miles!

STANDISH—Yes, Barbara. What wouldest thou?

BARBARA—How much longer is Garrett Foster to bide at Plymouth?

STANDISH—It would seem, Barbara, till Garrett Foster is pleased to take himself hence.

BARBARA—Weston's sick men whom we kept here to nurse, sail away this afternoon to their own colony at Wessagusett, is it not so?

STANDISH—And 'tis your wish that Garrett sail with them?

BARBARA—There is no reason that a lusty youth such as he should tarry here longer upon any score of sickness.

STANDISH—So you hold those rakeshames at Wessagusett good playfellows for a lusty youth? Eh, Barbara?

BARBARA—Since you'll have all my mind—I hold Garrett Foster not a fit playfellow for our Rose.

STANDISH—Rose, eh? So you think—

BARBARA—I think, for all I am angered with Rose that she doth so conduct her toward John Margeson and Miriam, still I do think she is at heart too good a lass for such a rapscallion as Garrett Foster.

STANDISH—Tut, tut! There's no harm in Garrett. Hath he not labored faithfully amongst us these months? And he handles sword and musket as tidily as any man in the colony—better by far than your worthy John Margeson. A good lad, with red blood in him!

BARBARA—But no good lad for Rose!

STANDISH—But, Bab—   *Rises*

BARBARA—Nay, I say! (*sings*)
>   Now the daylight fair is gone,
>   Lullaby, lullaby!
>   And the dark comes creeping on—
Are you not of my mind, Miles?

STANDISH—I must e'en make myself of thy mind, I take it, if I'm to have peace in my own house!

Though I'll tell thee again, I have a rare liking for Garrett. Something of a dare-devil, the lad may be, but I tell thee the dare-devils make the best soldiers and the best seamen——

BARBARA—And the best husbands, Miles? Eh, then?

STANDISH—How guessed you that, Puss?

BARBARA—I guessed it not. I know it—by experience.

STANDISH—Do you, you witch? And will you shut our Rose from this same blissful experience? What am I to read in that?

BARBARA—This, Miles: it taketh a discreet woman to live at peace with a dare-devil.

STANDISH—On my soul, you shall pay me for that self-praise!   *Kisses her*

Enter from the wood Philippe, carrying two rapiers.

PHILIPPE—Pardon me, Captain Standish. Do I come amiss?

STANDISH—Amiss? What should make you think so? May not a man kiss his wife, so it be not the Sabbath?

PHILIPPE—Nay, nay, I——

BARBARA—Were you seeking Rose, Philippe? She hath gone forth with Garrett to gather nuts.

PHILIPPE—To be sure, yes, I was seeking Rose. Did —did Miriam Chillingsley go with her?

BARBARA—Nay, Miriam kept the house.

PHILIPPE—She is not ill, good Mistress Standish?

BARBARA—Ill? Oh, no! Sit you down, Philippe.

PHILIPPE—Yea, an I may.   I'll wait till Rose comes.
Sits on stump, polishes rapiers

STANDISH—Thou'rt a good lad, Philippe.   'Tis seldom
I have seen a youth more devoted to his sister.

Enter from wood Aunt Resolute, leaning on a staff.

AUNT RESOLUTE—Devoted to his sister?   To his sister?   Ay, ay, surely!   What else should bring our
Philippe hither at all hours of the day, but devotion to
his sister?

Exit Standish into wood, laughing.

Yet of late, he hath been so often at our door, a sus-
picion is on me, he cometh not always to see his sister,
but to see—

PHILIPPE—(*in alarm*) Mistress Story!

AUNT RESOLUTE—Nay, 'tis time thou wert told it,
plump and fair—there's no hope for thee, lad!   There's
no hope for thee!

PHILIPPE—(*in agony*) Mistress Story!

AUNT RESOLUTE—No hope, I tell thee, no!   Youth-
ful as is my seeming, I have laid past such vanities as
wooing and wedding more years than one.

PHILIPPE—(*utterly amazed*) Mistress Story!

AUNT RESOLUTE—Nay, was it not a-wooing to me
that thou camest hither so oft, Philippe?

PHILIPPE—Mistress Story!   O Lord!   You—I—O,
Mistress Story!

AUNT RESOLUTE—Not I?   Well, well, how even a
woman of some experience may misread a youth.   Not

I, eh? (*Philippe shakes his head, smiling bashfully yet mischievously*) Well, mayhap 'twere best. For I take it a marriage with such disparity in years as ours would set all tongues a-wagging, even in Plymouth—ay, even in Plymouth!

PHILIPPE—(*with relief*) Mistress Story! *Kisses her hand*

AUNT RESOLUTE—Nay, nay! Not before others!

BARBARA—You are returned, good Aunt? And you enjoyed your walk in the forest? Sure, there never was a kinder day!

AUNT RESOLUTE—Enjoy? Enjoy? Good lack, I went not forth to seek enjoyment! There be but two things to do in this forsaken spot: sleep snug in your bed, or wake to be frightened nigh to death. I have slept my fill, and now I have been forth to take my daily frighting—and fright I found a plenty! Scarce set I forth, when behind a great oak tree—

BARBARA—Well?

AUNT RESOLUTE—I heard the rustle of an Indian's foot.

BARBARA—(*excitedly*) An Indian!

AUNT RESOLUTE—Nay, calm thee, good niece, calm thee! Methought 'twas an Indian, but when I did draw more close I saw 'twas naught but a chattering jackanapes of a squirrel. (*Philippe laughs, Barbara is much relieved*) Next as I strolled on, but new recovered from that terror, I heard a roaring, a most fearsome roaring, and a crashing in the thicket—

PHILIPPE—A crash? A roaring?

AUNT RESOLUTE—Ay.

PHILIPPE—What roared?

AUNT RESOLUTE—What but that son of Satan, the Governor's new bull calf? Ay, ay, I've had rare enjoyment in my walk abroad! A toad under every flower that I stooped to pick, a snake under every leaf—

PHILIPPE—(*polishing rapier, speaks as if to himself*) A snake? And under every leaf? Ay, verily, last night the Captain's brandy posset was uncommon strong! (*Aunt Resolute starts toward him with staff uplifted to strike*) Back! What is that moving under yonder leaf? (*Aunt Resolute shrieks and beats at the leaf*) Nay, 'twas but the wind that stirred the leaf! Oh, that posset, that posset!

AUNT RESOLUTE—Nay, I'll bide here no longer to be baited by a saucy fledgling. *Sits on porch, fanning herself*

　　Enter from the house Miriam, who is knitting at a stocking.

MIRIAM—Have they not yet returned, Mistress Standish?

AUNT RESOLUTE—They?

MIRIAM—Why, Rose and Garrett. Are they not returned?

BARBARA—As you see. But Philippe—

MIRIAM—(*carelessly*) Ah, good morrow, Philippe. (*to Barbara*) I have dropped this troublesome stitch.

BARBARA—Give it me. *Takes knitting, re-adjusts it*

　　Re-enter Standish, and stands watching Philippe.

MIRIAM—I wanted so to knit out this ball of yarn ere they come. Rose and Garrett and—and John Margeson are coming to crack nuts this afternoon, you understand.

PHILIPPE—Am not I bidden too, Miriam?

MIRIAM—(*carelessly*) Oh, yes!   *Knits*

STANDISH—A merry-making, is it? Then Julius Cæsar and I were best betake ourselves to quiet. You have polished my rapiers as I bade thee, lad?

PHILIPPE—Ay, sir, I trust they're bright to your mind. Yet I would work a breath longer at this rust-spot ere I bring them in. 'Tis vengeance slow to clear, this rust-spot.

STANDISH—'Twas vengeance hard to win, that rust-spot! He was a rare swordsman from whom I won that rust-spot.

MIRIAM—Captain! You do not mean that you—

STANDISH—I mean—Nay, there be tales not for a maid's hearing. See that you clear me the rust-spot, Phil.

Exit Standish into house.

PHILIPPE—(*goes to Miriam at L*) See how you drive the Captain hence, Miriam. Methinks you be somewhat bitter unto all men, save to John Margeson.

MIRIAM—Nay, how am I so? Pray you, Philippe, you are standing in my light.

PHILIPPE—(*moving aside*) I pray you, pardon me.

Enter Rose, running, from wood.

Rose—(*calling over her shoulder*) Ah, sluggard! I wagered I'd beat you to the house!

Enter Garrett, with bag of nuts.

Garrett—I ran weighted, Rose.

Rose—Not heavily weighted. (*takes bag, turns to others*) Look on this, and be pitiful. All the nuts we could find! (*Philippe drops rapiers on ground and takes bag of nuts*) And we searched to very weariness, and O, Philippe, Garrett fell from the top of a tree.

Barbara—You suffered no hurt, I trust?

Garrett—Not to my skin, mistress—that is indifferent thick.

Aunt Resolute—But so is not the sleeve of Philippe's second-best doublet, alack and alas! *Points at Garrett with her staff. Garrett puts his left arm behind him.*

Rose—(*going to Garrett*) Villain! Let me see! (*seizes his arm. A long tear in the sleeve is disclosed*) You did not tell me!

Garrett—I thought it best to break the news to you slowly and gently.

Philippe—Why, 'tis no great matter, Garrett. Rose can sew it up in the winking of an eye.

Rose—If Rose chooses, yes.

Garrett—Then pray you, choose.

Rose—Do you deserve so much of me?

Garrett—As much—and much more.

Rose—Saucebox! *Rose sits on stump, Garrett kneels by her, and she mends his sleeve.*

PHILIPPE—(*examining nuts*) There'll be a plenty when all's said, you see.

MIRIAM—And John Margeson promised to bring more.

AUNT RESOLUTE—And is it sure that John Margeson comes?

MIRIAM—Ay, so he promised.

AUNT RESOLUTE—And speedily?

MIRIAM—At any moment now.

AUNT RESOLUTE—Then I bid you all a fair good day!

Exit Aunt Resolute into house.

MIRIAM—I must knit out this ball of yarn ere they come.

PHILIPPE—They?

MIRIAM—Why, John is not yet here.

PHILIPPE—I know.

MIRIAM—Look forth to the forest, I pray you, and see if he is coming.

PHILIPPE—I will.

Exit Philippe into wood.

BARBARA—Miriam! If Philippe, for all he is but a lad, if it chanced—Say that he had a liking for you, that was bitter cruel of you.

MIRIAM—Philippe? Why Philippe is even as a brother unto me.

BARBARA—"As a brother!" 'Tis a world-wide word, that "as!"

GARRETT—(*to Rose*) I wonder who 'tis will mend my clothes at Wessagusett.   I shall miss you, Rose.

ROSE—Wonder, too, who will lend you clothes to mend, Garrett Foster! You'll miss my brother Philippe.

GARRETT—I shall miss you both, and sorely.

ROSE—The boat sails this afternoon for Wessagusett, doth it not?

GARRETT—Yes.

ROSE—And you sail in her?

GARRETT—That's what I wait to know.

ROSE—To know?

GARRETT—I have spoke with the Governor and the Captain.   They say if I live soberly as I have lived since—since I knew you, Rose, they will allot me a strip of land and I can settle here.   But it rests with you to say if I shall.   You know what I mean.

ROSE—I know.

    Re-enter Philippe.

PHILIPPE—Nay, Miriam, I see naught of John.

MIRIAM—Let him come now.   My morning's stent is knit out. (*rises*) Where shall I find more yarn, Mistress Standish?

BARBARA—(*rising*) I'll find it for you.

MIRIAM—And you, Philippe, will you begin to crack the nuts?

    Exeunt Barbara and Miriam into house.

      Philippe kneels on ground at L and cracks nuts

GARRETT—(*to Rose*) An't please you, you are sewing my sleeve down on my shirt-sleeve.

ROSE—I care not. (*breaks thread*) 'Tis done now.

GARRETT—Nay, 'tis not done yet. You are to answer me. (*confidently*) 'Tis not done!

ROSE—There, then! (*sticks needle into his arm, rises*) Is't done now?

GARRETT—A pest on your mischief!

PHILIPPE—Rose, what mischief are you doing?

ROSE—Oh, naught. Just setting finish to my work.

GARRETT—(*following her to porch*) Is that my answer? Is't so you set sharp finish to your work?

ROSE—(*at house-door*) That's one answer. And here's another! *Throws him a kiss. Garrett starts forward to seize Rose. She darts into house and closes door behind her*

GARRETT—(*in high spirits*) The last law repeals those that went before it, and the last answer—hey, Philippe? (*strips off his coat, sits by Philippe on ground*) What do you there, little brother? At your devotions?

PHILIPPE—Maybe, yes.

GARRETT—Who is the saint?

PHILIPPE—Tell me now, Garrett Foster, did you ever love a woman?

GARRETT—A dozen of 'em!

PHILIPPE—Nay, now, you're playing the fool. And I spoke in earnest.

GARRETT—I'm in no mood for earnest answers to-day, Philippe.

PHILIPPE—I'm sorry.   I sought your counsel.

GARRETT—My counsel?   A staid fellow like you ask counsel of me?   Faith, 'tis a red-letter day!   And you want instruction in the Art of Love?

PHILIPPE—Say a man hath an affection—

GARRETT—Nay, say Philippe de la Noye consumes with love!

PHILIPPE—For a certain woman—

GARRETT—Say, Miriam Chillingsley!

PHILIPPE—How did you guess?

GARRETT—I'm neither bat nor mole.

PHILIPPE—But none of the others, not even John Margeson, suspects—

GARRETT—Pest on your Margeson!   He'd never suspect aught.   It argues brains—this suspecting.   So you love her, Phil?

PHILIPPE—Ay.

GARRETT—Then tell her so.

PHILIPPE—Why, she'd rebuff me.

GARRETT—How do you know?

PHILIPPE—I can guess.

GARRETT—In any case, 'twould be civil to give the lady opportunity to speak her mind.

PHILIPPE—How would you go about to tell her?

GARRETT—Why, thus.   Come hither!   (*takes Philippe's hand*) Miriam, my sweetheart—

PHILIPPE—Deuce take it, man!   Let go my hand!

GARRETT—True, she might speak thus, were she coy, but, by the Lord, Phil, Miriam hath no such hand-grip as thine! Be quiet now. Here's more instruction. I would go on about as thus: You know that I love you, lass, else you've no eyes; and I know that you have an inclination unto me—

PHILIPPE—Yes, but I don't know!

GARRETT—Hold your tongue! You're to speak only when Miriam would speak. That you have an inclination unto me. Then come, clap hands and a bargain! And a kiss thereupon!

PHILIPPE—(*throwing him off*) Hold, hold! On your honor, would you go about so to woo a maid?

Re-enter Rose and pauses in door-way, unobserved.

GARRETT—(*rising*) Faith, yes! For, mark me, Philippe, 'tis the only way. Plague of your mewling, pining lovers, say I! The wenches like to be carried by storm. Knock at the door, hat in hand, and you may cool your heels on the door-stone four hours together. But up with your knee and burst in the door boldly, and—

PHILIPPE—Did you ever woo a maid in just that way, Garrett?

GARRETT—To be sure, yes, half a score of them!

ROSE—(*coming forward*) How many of the half score did accept you, Garrett?

GARRETT—(*dumbfounded*) Rose, you—

ROSE—The Captain would speak unto you, Philippe.

Exit Philippe into house.

GARRETT—(*trying to appear at ease*) You come in a good time, Rose.

ROSE—Good time for you or for me? (*Garrett starts toward her*) Nay, now, I must turn my hand to the wheel. (*sits at wheel*) So you sail this afternoon for Wessagusett?

GARRETT—Do I?

ROSE—What know I? I but know 'tis a fair day for a journey.

GARRETT—You were in a different mood when you went hence.

ROSE—Or I mistake, or so were you.

GARRETT—Are you angry because of those foolish brags I was vaporing to Philippe?

ROSE—So you do acknowledge at last that you are a braggart? Oh, the good, humble youth! Tut, tut! Never thrust out your lip like that, Garrett. It becomes you very ill.

GARRETT—You might spare jesting, Rose. (*goes toward her*) You know that I—

ROSE—(*putting wheel between them*) I'd best be prepared if you go about to up with your knee and burst in the door boldly.

GARRETT—(*angrily*) The devil! *Sits on stump R*

ROSE—Truly, a proper patron saint for your fearsome style of wooing. Begin now! I'm fortified! (*after a moment, sings*)

> And now you're sulking, sulking, sulking,
> And now you're sulking, my good man!

GARRETT—You call for music, mistress? Listen, then! (*sings*)

> "Shall a woman's virtues move
> Me to perish for her love?
> Or her well deservings known,
> Make me quite forget mine own?"

ROSE—Rarely sung, Garrett! Only you flatted that last note. You'd best sing it again till you be perfect. Come, again! Again!

GARRETT—(*crosses to her, sings*)

> "If she slight me when I woo,
> I can scorn and let her go.
> If she be not fit for me,
> What care I for whom she be?"

Enter John from wood, with several ears of corn.

JOHN—Give you good day!

ROSE—Oh, you are come at last? (*runs to him*) Nay, fling by your hat, and be you welcome! Such dull company as I am pining in! Nay, I'm your servant ever for this release.

JOHN—I scarce dared hope for such a welcome, Rose. Give you good day, Foster.

GARRETT—(*shortly*) Good day, sir. *Sits sulkily on step of porch.*

ROSE—Fie, fie! Where are your manners, Garrett? John, have you brought the nuts you promised?

JOHN—Nay, something better than that. Look you, 'tis a kind of corn I got of the Indians. If you fry it, 'twill turn white and be most dainty to eat.

Rose—Truly? Thou art a rare lad, John! Here, Philippe, quickly!

Re-enter Philippe.

Wood, and a spark to't! I'll run within for the skillet. *Philippe gathers loose twigs and makes a little fire at R.*

John—Come, Foster, for all the corn be mine, will you not at least look thereon?

Garrett—No.

Rose—I prithee, speak not of corn to Garrett. Since last August it hath been a tender subject with him.

Exit Rose, laughing, into house.

John—(*laughing*) I wonder not, in truth!

Garrett—Do you mind, Margeson, there be some tendernesses 'tis best not to touch with a rude hand—lest tenderness turn tough!

John—And what tenderness of thine am I to keep hands off, Garrett Foster? Thy tenderness for corn, or thy tenderness for—Roses?

Garrett—Keep a maid's name from men's quarrels, you—

Philippe—Peace, you firebrands! Will you turn the autumn woods redder still? Peace! The maids are here.

Re-enter Rose, who carries a long-handled skillet, and Miriam, with a skein of yarn.

Rose—Who cried "quarrel"? Sure, one cried "quarrel" as we came! A rare hour to quarrel, with such toys at hand to say whose quarrel's right! *Points to rapiers*

MIRIAM—Ah, Rose, a wicked jest! Good day unto you, John. What hold you there?

ROSE—Nay, bear him the skillet, and he will show thee magic with what he holds.

MIRIAM—I may help you, John?

JOHN—Nay, let me not break your labor with the yarn you carry. 'Twas Rose that promised. *Miriam sighs and turns away. John goes to fire, gives skillet to Philippe to hold, and shells corn into it. Garrett rises and goes quickly to Rose.*

GARRETT—Rose!

ROSE—(*back to him*) Um-m!

GARRETT—In an hour they hoist sail for Wessagusett. And I wait your answer.

ROSE—Still waiting that answer? I thought you gave me mine long since, that song—

GARRETT—I was angered. I meant it not. Ah, Rose, sweetheart, I meant it not.

ROSE—If I meant it not, I would not sing that song. 'Tis scarce a pretty song.

GARRETT—If you like it not, I will forget it and forever. You see, I am obedient.

ROSE—Miriam, suffer Garrett hold that yarn for you since he desires it.

GARRETT—But I—

ROSE—Let me see if you be so obedient.

MIRIAM—Here, Garrett, if you will.   *Sits on porch*

GARRETT—(*bitterly*) It gladdens my heart to serve you.   *Sits near Miriam, holds yarn for her to wind*

ROSE—How speed you there, John?   *Saunters to fire*

JOHN—The better for your coming!   *Rises, the ear of corn in his hand.*

ROSE—La, la! What a clumsy compliment you make me there! And old—so old as Methuselah, the father of lies.

JOHN—Nay, the Scriptures tell us—

ROSE—Oh! Then was he not the father of lies? (*Looks toward Garrett. Garrett has turned his back toward Rose, and is making pretense of interested chat with Miriam*) Still, some one must have fathered them, for in the world there be lies a plenty!

MIRIAM—(*laughing*) O, Garrett! What a droll tale you tell! I ne'er knew you merrier.

GARRETT—(*boisterously*) Why, mistress, 'tis an afternoon for merry-making!

ROSE—(*turns to John, with hysterical simulation of merriment*) Look you how busy they be, Miriam and Garrett, and so happy! Do not your Scriptures say, 'tis labor brings contentment, eh, John Margeson? Let us not be idle, then. Give me hither that ear of corn.

JOHN—Nay, 'tis too harsh and stubborn work for your little tender hands.   *Holds the ear of corn above his head*

ROSE—Ah, *vaurien*! *Reaches for the ear which John holds. A laughing struggle between them. Garrett watches Rose and John, frowning and wincing at the sight.*

ROSE—Nay, but I will!   Oh, giant that you are!
Give it me, I say!   Philippe!   Ungenerous, why will
you not help?   Ah, but I will have it!   *Voilà!* (*waves
ear of corn triumphantly*)   Now shall you see! (*tries to
shell corn with her fingers*)   Oh!   'Tis of a toughness!
Sits on stump

JOHN—Let me—

ROSE—Nay, let be!   Give me your knife hither, Philippe!   Your knife, I say!

PHILIPPE—(*hands her his knife, in a warning voice*)
Have a care, sister!   Keen-edged tools, they are not
pretty toys for a maid to sport with—nor always are
they safe.   I warn you!   Have a care!

ROSE—(*aside to him*)   Safe!   What care I now for
safety?   What care I now for aught dull—or honest
—this afternoon of—merry-making? (*Garrett still pretends to be busied with Miriam*)   Behold me now, good
John!   All armed to the encounter!   *Starts to cut corn
from cob.*

JOHN—A fair warrior, in good truth!

ROSE—(*watching Garrett*)   Ah, think you so, John?
(*cuts unheedingly and wounds her hand*)   Oh!

GARRETT—Rose!   *Starts to her*

PHILIPPE—I warned you!   Rose!

ROSE—(*piteously*)   My hand doth bleed!

MIRIAM—Oh!   The sight of blood!   *Half faint, she
clings to Garrett, holding him back from Rose.*

GARRETT—Rose, let me look—

ROSE—(*looks at Garrett, standing beside Miriam, then deliberately holds out her hurt hand to John*) Nay, Garrett, Miriam doth need your kindness! I pray you, dear John, bind up the hurt for me. *Garrett turns and goes slowly toward the porch, where he stands snapping a twig between his fingers, his eyes on the ground.*

MIRIAM—(*amazed and reproachful*) O, Rose! What is it that you do?

ROSE—(*to John*) 'Tis not a deep hurt?

PHILIPPE—Naught is yet hurt that cannot heal. But hurt no more!

JOHN—Leave it to me, Philippe! (*Binds up Rose's hand*) You trust your hand unto me, Rose?

ROSE—(*curtly*) Yea, I trust you—with my finger-tips!

MIRIAM—(*going to porch*) Garrett! *Touches his shoulder*

GARRETT—(*roughly*) Have done!

MIRIAM—I pray you—we two, we are but sorry spoil-sports here— (*half crying*) I pray you, come in!

GARRETT—Ay, 'tis the harder for you, little wench! For I have comfort yet in store—a man's comfort. Go your ways in!

> *Exit Miriam into house, crying softly.*

I have a man's comfort! *Sits on step of porch, fingering one of the rapiers.*

JOHN—There! (*finishes bandage*) Is't not fairly done.

ROSE—Ay, fairly.

JOHN—The surgeon's fee! *Kisses her hand. Rose starts up, half frightened at what she has roused in him.*

PHILIPPE—Hey, John, to your work! I labor to no profit, if you give me not soon fresh store of corn. Catch, lad!   *Tosses John an unhusked ear of corn*

JOHN—Ay, let us be busy, Rose. What said you? "Labor breeds contentment"? Look you, now Garrett sits idle, he hath fallen to sulking.

GARRETT—(*looks up, testing point of rapier with his hand*) Nay, I am not sulking—nor am I altogether idle. *John tears off last husk of corn.*

ROSE—Ah, look! The ear of corn! 'Tis red—a fearsome color—the hue of blood!

JOHN—The red ear! Know you the custom of the red ear?

ROSE—What custom?

JOHN—Amongst the savages, the warrior that finds the red ear may clasp and claim what maid he will. (*Garrett springs up*) And we, surely we should follow so good a custom!   *Catches Rose in his arms*

ROSE—(*in terror*) Ah, John! Let be!

GARRETT—(*with an inarticulate cry*) You dog! *Crosses and strikes John so that he reels back.*

ROSE—(*hiding her face*) What have I done! What have I done!

PHILIPPE—Edged tools! I warned you!

JOHN—A blow—and from you, you unwhipped thief!

GARRETT—There is a way to wipe out blows. Come, Bully Margeson! Smooth down your cuffs again, man. I'll teach you how gentlemen fight. *Catches up rapiers*

JOHN—The rogue!   What means he?   Fight?   And here?

ROSE—Ah, no!   Not here!   Philippe!

PHILIPPE—Too late, I say!   Keep back!

GARRETT—(*throws rapier at John's feet*) Your sword, Master Margeson!

JOHN—Nay, I be no cut-throat to have a hand in such bloody—

ROSE—I knew it, little brother!   There'll be no fight! No fight!

JOHN—Give me the rapier.   (*throws off his coat*) 'Tis you who have bred this crime, mistress.

GARRETT—(*seizing Rose's arm*) You jade! You jade! When I have done you shall kiss me o' the mouth for this!

ROSE—I will kiss the better man.

GARRETT—Then you will kiss me.   *Garrett almost flings Rose aside, and engages with John.   The sun is now near to setting behind the autumn trees.   Only a little light is caught and held by the flickering rapiers.*

PHILIPPE—Oh, you fools!   Put up!   Put up, I say!

ROSE—(*crouching against the porch, almost beside herself*) Oh, what did I say?   They are fighting—they are fighting for me—for me!   O, God!   Stop them!   Stop them!   Philippe!   Philippe!

PHILIPPE—Too late, I say!   Too late!

Re-enter Miriam from house.

MIRIAM—O, John! John! John Margeson will be killed! Help! Help! Help!

Re-enter Barbara.

BARBARA—A duel! (*calls into house*) Miles! Miles!

Re-enter Standish.

STANDISH—Put up, you fools, put up! I'll hang you both!

ROSE—Hang! And I—Oh, stop! stop! stop! *Flings herself madly between the combatants.*

PHILIPPE—Are you gone mad? *Philippe flings Rose aside and himself, by the impetus, breaks through the rapiers, staggers, and recovers himself at back. He draws out his handkerchief and holds it to his side, staunching the blood and every moment growing weaker. No one heeds him. Barbara is entirely occupied with Miriam, who clings to her, half hysterical.*

GARRETT—(*to John, still fighting mad*) Have at you, now! *As they engage again, Garrett wounds John slightly in the arm.*

STANDISH—Stand where you are—on your life! *Garrett and John lower their rapiers.*

ROSE—O, Captain! Captain!

STANDISH—Who began this? (*There is an instant's pause. Then John lifts his rapier and with it points at Garrett*) You, Garrett Foster? (*Garrett raises his eyes, meets the Captain's glance, and lets his eyes fall again*) Here is no place for brawlers. I put sentence of banishment upon you. Never show your face again within the Plymouth settlement.

Rose—(*wildly*) Banish him? No, no! O, Captain! 'Twas I stirred them to their quarrel—I—O, Garrett! Garrett!

Philippe—(*coming forward, faintly*) I pray you, Captain! Garrett—do not—   *Staggers*

Standish—(*catching Philippe*) Lad! What's wrong?
                                Helps him to sit on stump

Rose—Philippe! O, my brother!

Philippe—Nay, 'tis nothing! I came between them —Rose—Rose was— *Falls back, fainting, against Standish's arm.*

Rose—Oh! *Throws herself down on her knees by Philippe*

Garrett—Rose! Forgive—

Standish—Go!

Rose—What have I done? O, dear God! What have I done? *Rose buries her head, sobbing, on Philippe's knees. Garrett turns and goes slowly into wood. John, with his hand pressed to his wounded arm, watches him go*

CURTAIN

Act III The Red Light on the Snow

ACT III

Scene:—SAME AS ACT I. Candles lighted on table and chimneypiece. Through the windows can be seen the dark night sky, and a few keen, wintry stars.

At rise of curtain, Barbara sits on settle, Miriam at her feet, with her head resting on Barbara's knee. Rose at window. Aunt Resolute by fire, knitting.

BARBARA—Rose! Rose!

ROSE—What is't? I thought you all asleep.

BARBARA—Miriam is dozing—

MIRIAM—(*sleepily*) Indeed, no!

BARBARA—Rest you still, child! Can you see naught, Rose?

ROSE—Nay, all is dark at the landing. And John Margeson promised me so soon as the shallop touched the shore he would show a lanthorn there.

BARBARA—A good lad!

AUNT RESOLUTE—Ay, good at holding a torch to other men's triumphs!

BARBARA—Nay, 'tis not his fault that he had no part in this expedition to Manomet; all the settlement could not share therein.

ROSE—My brother Philippe went.

MIRIAM—(*rousing up*) What said you of Philippe?

ROSE—The truth, for I spoke only good of him.

AUNT RESOLUTE—What time o' night is it, niece?

BARBARA—Past mid-evening, I judge, and nipping cold, I know. I ne'er have known a night in March so bitter.

MIRIAM—How they must be suffering in the shallop!

ROSE—Light, ho! Light, ho!

BARBARA—They're coming? They're coming? *Barbara and Miriam go to window.*

ROSE—Thrice waved! 'Tis they returned, and cold and hungry, too. Come, stir, stir, Miriam! Look to the soup if it boil.   *Miriam runs to fire*

BARBARA—Let us show them a light also. *Takes candle from table.*

ROSE—They'll need no light to find their way hither. Hark! (*The tramp of feet is heard in the snow without*) Here cometh one already!

Enter C Standish, in corselet and helmet.

BARBARA—Miles! O, my husband!

STANDISH—(*kissing her*) Safe back again, you see, Bab, a bit frosty, but hale else. Faith, you're all astir!

ROSE—Where should we be, Captain?

STANDISH—You might be sleeping snugly, as we found the watchers in the Common House but now.

ROSE—Sleeping? Margeson and all?

AUNT RESOLUTE—Margeson if any, I'll wager me!

STANDISH—Why so fierce? Their keeping awake profited no one.

ROSE—True enough, Captain, though you might say kinder.

BARBARA—What success had you in your expedition, Miles?

STANDISH—Why, fair success. But preserve me from ever making another expedition with the Wessagusett men!

BARBARA—Such ill comrades?

STANDISH—I would not ask for worse. Still, we have secured the corn and some beans.

BARBARA—And what of the Indians, Miles? Are they friendly?

STANDISH—Friendly or not, what matters it?

BARBARA—Indians have arrows, Miles.

STANDISH—Ay, and the Plymouth men have bullets. (*laughs*) The Indians are friendly.

MIRIAM—Will you eat of the soup now, Captain Standish?

STANDISH—Presently, cousin. I'll shift off this armor first.

BARBARA—I'll light you hence.

Exit Barbara R, with candle.

ROSE—(*detaining Standish*) Captain Standish, have you heard—is there any news maybe—come from Wessagusett?

STANDISH—No good news, lass. 'Tis an ill end their settlement is rushing to. They began with robbing the savages, and now the savages rob them, and they be so weak they must pocket it up. 'Tis a shame to their English blood! They are living like dogs.

ROSE—All of them? Oh! All of them?

STANDISH—So it was for one man, and not the whole settlement, you questioned me? Do you think that man hath proved worthy of the liking of honest folk? Nay, forget him, lass, forget him!

Exit Standish R.

MIRIAM—You still can have a tenderness for that wicked man?

ROSE—Wicked? Sure, 'twas not your brother he near killed.

MIRIAM—Nay, but he hurt John Margeson sorely.

AUNT RESOLUTE—Not sorely enough! 'Twas the worse news I heard of the whole clamjamfry when I woke from my nap that he hurt not Margeson sorely!

ROSE—Ay, John recovered. All is as it was before, save that Garrett Foster is sent away.

MIRIAM—Nay, comfort you, Rose, if you need comfort. It may be he will return again.

ROSE—O, Miriam Chillingsley! Who asks him to return? Sure, I do not. Was it not I sent him hence? Did I not say I wished never to see him—

Enter Philippe C, in buff jacket and high boots.

PHILIPPE—Never see whom, Rose? Not me, I pray!

ROSE—Philippe! You've come back safe? (*embraces him*) Ah! How cold you are!

PHILIPPE—I'll be warm speedily.

AUNT RESOLUTE—Come hither to the fire, lad.

PHILIPPE—(*sees Miriam and starts to her*) Why, Miriam!

MIRIAM—(*with a bowl in her hand*) Oh, gently, gently! I'll spill the soup.

PHILIPPE—What matters the soup?

ROSE—'Tis not your soup to spill, sir, 'tis the Captain's.

PHILIPPE—You are looking kindly to the Captain's welfare, Miriam. Have you done naught for me?

MIRIAM—Yea, indeed, there is soup and to spare for you, Philippe. Rose will surely give it unto you.

Exit Miriam R.

ROSE—Yea, that I will. Sit you down, Philippe, and I'll fetch it you.

PHILIPPE—(*sitting by table*) Nay, I am not hungry.

AUNT RESOLUTE—Good lack, but he's young!

ROSE—Yet but now—Hey, presto! It's a tricksy appetite you have, Philippe.   *Goes to him at table*

PHILIPPE—In any case, 'tis gone.

ROSE—Unless Miriam return to serve you, eh? Listen to me, Philippe, listen to me. I bade thee brother Miriam, but I did not bid thee be more brotherly to her than to thine own sister.

PHILIPPE—(*taking her hands*) I would not be her brother for the world, Rose. Fret not yourself for that, for I say it from my heart.

ROSE—Philippe, you are laughing at me.

PHILIPPE—Nay, I protest to you—

ROSE—In the depth of your eyes you are laughing. Let me go! (*tries to pull away from him*) I hate you! Let me go!

PHILIPPE—Come, come, be not angry with me, Rose. Be your own dear self again and answer me soberly, for there are a many things I have to ask you.

ROSE—Ask me? Of what?

PHILIPPE—Hath John Margeson been hither often these last days?

AUNT RESOLUTE—Cheer thee! He is under foot most times o' day.

PHILIPPE—With whom doth he talk?

ROSE—With whomsoever is foolish enough to listen.

PHILIPPE—Is—is Miriam ever thus foolish?

ROSE—I thought you held Miriam discreet.

PHILIPPE—I—I respect Miriam. I like not to see her pining. Doth all her love still turn to Margeson? Say true, sister!

ROSE—Truly, the soup is boiling over! *Tries to run to fire.*

PHILIPPE—(*staying her*) These days when we have been storm-bound, when you knew we were in peril on the sea, did—did she speak aught—of us, Rose? Have we—have I been at all in her thoughts? Tell me, sweetheart sister, tell me!

ROSE—I see not what concern of yours it is, Philippe.

PHILIPPE—I would fain know if I have been at all in her thoughts. Come, honey, answer me.

ROSE—You are far too young for such matters, little brother.   *Breaks away from him*

PHILIPPE—(*after a moment*) As you will. What shall I do with this letter, Rose?

ROSE—What letter?

PHILIPPE—A letter for you I have here.

Rose—For me? Oh! For me? From Wessagusett?

Philippe—One of the settlers who joined our expedition gave it me. I think he said 'twas from Garrett Foster.

Rose—(*running to him*) Oh, give it me, give it me, Philippe!

Philippe—Now I see not what concern of yours it is, my Rose.

Rose—Philippe de la Noye, give me my letter!

Philippe—You are far too young for such matters, little sister. I'll bear it to the Captain.

Rose—Oh! Philippe! Philippe! Come back! Come back! What is it that you want me to say of Miriam? Give me my letter. I'll tell you anything.

Philippe—Hath she thought of me?

Rose—Oh, she hath lain awake all night and gone quite without food. Give me my letter.

Philippe—Nay, answer me in earnest.

Rose—Nay, 'tis mostly earnest. The day it stormed so bitterly, she wept, though she wished me not to know. She hath had no more than a good morrow for John Margeson since you set sail. Now give me my letter, dear, sweet Philippe, give me my letter!

Philippe—Nay, dear, sweet Rose, there is one thing else you must do ere you have it.

Rose—Aught you will, but be brisk, be brisk!

Philippe—Will you find pretext to send Miriam hither unto me, and quickly ere my courage ooze away?

Rose—I will, I will!   I'll have her here though I fright my guardian angel with my lying. (*snatches letter*) You rogue!   'Twould serve you rightly if I broke promise with you! (*opens letter*)   O, me!   O, me!   I cannot read this devilish English hand!

Philippe—Maybe I might—

Rose—Maybe you mightn't!   I'll take it unto Aunt Resolute!   O, sweet Aunt Resolute, wake up! *Shakes her*

Aunt Resolute—Eh?

Rose—Come thou within and read to me my letter.

Aunt Resolute—Within?   Nay, 'tis too far from the fire.

Rose—Nay, sure, 'tis warm within!   Are not the Captain and Mistress Standish biding there?

Aunt Resolute—And doth a man in love with his second wife know if the fire burn or no?

Rose—Nay, indeed, I feel good warmth from within.

Aunt Resolute—Ay, good warmth, with thy letter on thy breast!   I've no such make-cheer to fright the rheumatics.

Rose—Oh, but Aunt Resolute, you read so beautifully —sweet Aunt Resolute!

Aunt Resolute—Well, well, I'll come!   I'll come!

Exeunt Rose and Aunt Resolute R.

Philippe—Dear Rose!   She doth love him, whether or no.   He was a rare lad, Garrett Foster.   Perhaps, after all, some part of that advice of his was sound.   A bit more courage—and give the lass a chance to speak her mind. (*starts to door R boldly, changes his mind, comes slowly back to fire*) Foster's advice—good advice it sounded—yet Foster's way of wooing sped but ill with Rose! And if it fare so with Miriam! Lord! Lord! what a thing it is to be afraid! I think I ne'er before was afraid in all my life! Now if Miriam were but an Indian with a tomahawk—Hark! Is it she? Now Heaven forbid that she be coming now, so soon— an hour hence—a half hour hence—

Re-enter Miriam.

Ah! Good even, Miriam.

MIRIAM—You sent for me, Rose said.

PHILIPPE—Rose told you that I sent for you? When I did but bid the jade send you hither that I might pretend I met you by mistake!

MIRIAM—Philippe!

PHILIPPE—Lord! That was a sweet beginning!

MIRIAM—Nay, if Rose erred and you want me not—

PHILIPPE—Want you? I ne'er knew what 'twas to want until I wanted you. Have you no word of welcome for me?

MIRIAM—You are welcome home. Sure, that you know without my saying.

PHILIPPE—Things that people know are yet ofttimes sweet to hear.

MIRIAM—Yea, I can well believe it.   *Goes to window*

PHILIPPE—Ah, you watch for Margeson.

MIRIAM—Why should I watch for him? He is Rose's lover, not mine.

PHILIPPE—Nay, forgive me.

MIRIAM—There is naught to forgive. Why should you not speak of John? He is naught unto me.

PHILIPPE—(*going to her*) You mean—

MIRIAM—Yea, I mean it in truth. For I— (*embarrassed, looks out of window*) For he— Ah! What was that?

PHILIPPE—Where?

MIRIAM—There, yonder, the red light on the snow.

PHILIPPE—Nay, 'tis nothing. A light from the sky, we saw it yesternight.

MIRIAM—Oh, I like it not. 'Tis fearsome—'tis like witch-play.

PHILIPPE—Nay, look not forth. Come hither to the fire.

MIRIAM—(*sits on settle*) I remember it. When I was a child, they used to tell me that that red light presaged war and the shedding of blood.

PHILIPPE—Heaven forbid!

MIRIAM—Tell me, Philippe, tell me true—somewhat of Captain Standish's talk I overheard but now, somewhat touching the savages. Sure, you met with no unfriendliness among the savages?

PHILIPPE—Why, no, Miriam.

MIRIAM—You are cheating me because you think me afraid. Tell me truly, Philippe, who is the Indian Wituwamat the Captain spoke of?

PHILIPPE—Why, 'tis just when we were at Manomet, this Wituwamat of the Massachusetts tribe came in unto the Captain and delivered a long speech we none of us could understand. Yea, and he looked scornfully upon us, but looks hurt no man and—You must not be afraid, indeed, indeed you must not be afraid, Miriam, sweetheart! (*gasps, stops*) It doth not offend you that I—called you sweet—that I— (*sits by her*) It doth not offend— (*aside*) Mayhap 'tis the moment! A bit more courage, and beat in the door boldly! *Very timidly puts his arm about Miriam.*

MIRIAM—(*indignantly*) Philippe!

PHILIPPE—(*drawing away to the far end of settle, angrily*) Beat in the door boldly! Verily, that Garrett Foster was a fool! Now you're angered, Miriam. And I— I— Ah, well, I cannot doubt 'tis that your thoughts are still with John Margeson.

MIRIAM—No, I tell you, no! I have never given a thought to John Margeson, not one, not since—*Hesitates*

PHILIPPE—(*eagerly*) Since when?

MIRIAM—Now do you think the heart of a maid doth keep a calendar of days or of weeks?

PHILIPPE—Ah, why will you tease me? Why can't you, like a sweet maid, make it easier for me to tell you that I love you? You know I want to tell you. You know I—I don't dare tell you—I know not how to tell you I love you—I have had no experience in such matters.

MIRIAM—(*pleased, turning to him*) Truly, Philippe?

PHILIPPE—Ay, truly! Why, I've never in my life so much as kissed any maid save Rose, my sister—

MIRIAM—How good you—

PHILIPPE—You see, there's so devilish little chance here for a lad to learn kissing. There are naught but staid and married women here in Plymouth town.

MIRIAM—(*vexed, turning away*) O, Philippe!

PHILIPPE—Now you won't look at me! You're not even listening! Oh, there's the devil in women!

MIRIAM—(*turns to him in horror*) Philippe!

PHILIPPE—(*seizing her hands as she turns*) Ay, that's better—that's much better! Now look at me—and tell me—Do you—May I—O, Lord! Why won't you give me one word of help?

MIRIAM—Mistress Standish says 'tis not seemly a maid show her love for a man till he hath—he hath—

PHILIPPE—But I *hath*. I would say I—I can't find the word to—

MIRIAM—Is a lad's love best told—in words?

PHILIPPE—You mean—Lord! You mean that I may —that I—O, Miriam! *Catches and kisses her rapturously*

BARBARA—(*within*) Patiently, patiently, Rose! *As Philippe starts to kiss Miriam again,*

    Re-enter Barbara and Rose.

Philippe tries to kiss Miriam, but does not quite dare, lest the others see him. Miriam, who is quite sure they will be seen, protests in dumb-show.

ROSE—Sit you down here, Mistress Standish. Nay, but Aunt Resolute had scarce begun my reading when she cried out on the cold and did scurry to her blankets. Here still, Philippe? Run hence, I pray you. Can you not talk unto the Captain?

PHILIPPE—That I will, and very gladly.   *Rises*

ROSE—Philippe!   *Points to Miriam*

PHILIPPE—Come, I wish you more than Rose, and she needs me not. Come, Miriam.

    Exeunt Philippe and Miriam R.

ROSE—Now read me my letter, sweet Mistress Standish. (*kneels by Barbara*) Oh, read! read!

BARBARA — Flurry me not, you giddy-pate! 'Tis a task for me to read writing, and this is ill writ indeed.

ROSE—Nay, I am sure 'tis very good writing.

BARBARA—Then why read you it not?

ROSE—'Tis only ill writing like mine own I can read. This is too good for my reading. Oh, haste, haste! What saith he?

BARBARA—(*reading*) "Good Mistress—"

ROSE—He might have said "Good Rose!" "Dear Rose"—that would have been yet seemlier.

BARBARA—"It hath been in my mind to write you even since the day I went from Plymouth."

ROSE—Sure, his mind shuts with lock and key, since nothing in comes out.

BARBARA—"But at the first I dared not, and still when I heard Philippe was recovered, I dared not."

ROSE—Out on him for a coward!

BARBARA—"I know not how 'tis I have ventured it now, unless it be—" Verily, he hath so blotted it hereabouts 'twill need a better eye than mine to unravel it.

ROSE—Oh, try, try! I must know "unless it be" what! Read me that "unless"!

BARBARA—"Unless it be—"

ROSE—Hurry! Hurry!

BARBARA—"I know not how 'tis I have ventured it now, unless it be—it be—" Ah! "Unless it be that I know where love hath ceased, pity may be."

ROSE—Love hath ceased? Love hath ceased?

BARBARA—"Forgive me, then, for that I hurt Philippe. I had not entered on the quarrel had I known your heart then as well as I know it now."

ROSE—Doth he know it?

BARBARA—"But it was all true and earnest, what I said that day, though you would not believe it."

ROSE—Ah, but I did believe it! How else, since that day, hath my heart ached all day long?

BARBARA—"The rumor comes from Plymouth that in the spring you will wed John Margeson—"

ROSE—He could write that? He could believe that?

BARBARA—"If you hold him the better man and love him—"

ROSE—But I don't, I don't! Here he insults my taste with all else!

BARBARA—"I pray you may be happy. And in your happiness you must cease to hate me and try to forgive."

ROSE—Forgive? I did it long since.

BARBARA—"I can stay for no answer, for the chance hath just come to me to go north to Monhegan. I shall join the fishing fleet and work my way to England."

ROSE—To England? To England?

BARBARA—"I shall never again vex you, and so make an end of ill will. Your assured faithful servant, Garrett Foster."

ROSE—(*as if dazed*) He hath gone! He hath gone! Oh! Oh! (*hides her face against Barbara's knee*) I said —I would lead John Margeson a dance. 'Tis mine own happiness I have danced down—mine own happiness and a brave man's heart!

BARBARA—Rose! My little Rose! Indeed, for all your folly, you have not deserved this bitter pain.

ROSE—He hath gone! He will not stay for an answer! (*starts up, hysterically*) What right had he? Nay, I will marry John Margeson then. I will not have Garrett Foster find that he judged me wrong. I will marry John Margeson!

BARBARA—Rose, what are you saying? You mad child! What are you saying?

ROSE—Have you not always praised John? Do you not counsel me to marry him? An honest, discreet youth, and I can have him for the asking! Nay, I can have him without the asking. His is no dear price.

BARBARA—(*goes to Rose, takes her in her arms*) Nay, it is your life, my Rose, my poor, poor little Rose, that you are binding, never to bloom loose in sun and wind again.   Ay, listen, dear! The happiest wife—and that, God knows, am I!—hath moments when—Ah, my Rose, read your letter yet again—and again, ere—

ROSE—What, what! You are not speaking for Garrett Foster? Nay, I care not for him nor for his letter, save that I shall marry John Margeson, I tell you, even as Master Foster doth advise.

STANDISH—(*within*) Barbara!   Here, Barbara!

BARBARA—I must go, my Rose, for an instant. There, I pray you, calm your mood and bethink yourself.   O, my dear, this is a long doing.   Ere you do it, think—and pray!

STANDISH—(*within*) Barbara!

BARBARA—I come, Miles!   I come!

   Exit Barbara R.

ROSE—Nay, I be calm enough to take the good advice my friends have proffered.   Sure, so good a friend as Garrett Foster must know!

   Enter John C, in military dress.

Ah-h! There is a proverb apt for this coming of thine, John.   Speak of the— Tut, tut! The end is not so flattering as the beginning.   Yet 'tis apt!

JOHN—Are you in one of your mad moods to-night?

ROSE—Nay, I am very sane, more sane than e'er before, so prudent folk would say.

JOHN—Why, so 'tis well.   For 'tis of a serious matter I come hither to speak to-night.

ROSE—(*with rising hysteria*) A serious matter? Nay, though it be serious, yet tell it with a merry face.   I will not have grave looks to-night, I tell you—I will not!   I will not!   Wherefore should I not be merry? I've had such gay news!   Why do you stand dumb, John Margeson?   Talk to me, good, ill, I care not what, only talk—talk!

JOHN—Would you have me break in upon you?

ROSE—Oh, ever your brave Sunday manners, John! And ever that long, long Sunday face!   Nay, look for once, just once, as men look o' weekdays.   What, ceremony still?   Well, then, there's my ceremonious curtsy to requite it.   And I should have a Sunday cap. (*snatches down cap from its hook, and puts it on*) V'la, your servant!   Is this brave enough to deserve your serious matter?   Serious?   La, la!   Tell it me now, good, grave John.   Is't Indians?   Is't a ship of war come from New Amsterdam?   Is the Governor fallen in an apoplexy?

JOHN—Truly, there are times I believe I like you in your wanton moods.

ROSE—My wanton moods are over-flattered, John. John!   Did any one ever call you "Jack"?   "Jack Margeson"!

JOHN—Nay, but you might call me that.

ROSE—Fortune, I thank thee! (*throws aside cap*) And what will you call me?

JOHN—Rose, I would call you—wife.

ROSE—Verily and indeed! Have you not said somewhat like to this ere now?

JOHN—Make an end of jesting, Rose. It has gone too far. The gossips have fast coupled our names—

ROSE—Coupled our names? Ours!

JOHN—Ay, since the ill affair with that son of perdition—

ROSE—Son of perdition? Ah, to be sure, you must mean that young man Foster—ay, Garrett Foster, he that gave you so sore an overthrow last summer.

JOHN—And had he not fled, like the outlawed villain that he was, the whipping-post was the least our law held in store for him.

ROSE—Oh, he hath no fear of your law—he hath now no concern for the colony or aught that is in it! Sure, this is not your grave matter—that Garrett Foster is a son of perdition? Tell me news! Tell me news!

JOHN—Is it not grave enough that I prayed you but now to marry me?

ROSE—Marry you!

JOHN—I stand as well as any man in the colony. I can care for you as well—

ROSE—And love me as well? Look me in the eyes and answer me that, John Margeson!

JOHN—Surely, I can love you well, Rose—so that you love me well.

Rose—Yes, yes. So that I love you well!

John—You'll marry me, then? 'Tis said?

Rose—Ay! Oh, let me say it quickly! I'll marry you, I tell you, I'll marry you! Are you content?

Philippe—(*within*) Good night to you, Captain!

Re-enter Philippe and Miriam R.

Philippe—Ah, John, do you bear me company down the hill? *Speaks with Miriam, bidding her good night in dumb-show.*

John—Good even then, Rose. And—my right.
Draws her to him

Rose—Ay, your right! *Very quiet and white she raises her face and with a little shudder receives his kiss.*

Philippe—Rose!

Rose—John and I have plighted troth, Philippe. Good night to you.

Exit John C.

Philippe—You—to John Margeson? Rose! After all you have said?

Rose—After all I have said. I—to John Margeson.

Philippe—(*angrily*) Good night!

Exit Philippe C. Miriam stands in door to watch him go.

Rose—Philippe! O, my brother! (*she strikes her hand against her lips*) His right! His right—forever— when he will—past my denying! Oh! Oh! *Sits on settle.*

MIRIAM—(*turning from door*) Dear Rose!

ROSE—Shut the door! Close and quick! I'm cold! I'm deathly cold!

MIRIAM—Ay, sure, 'tis a bitter night. Yet you should be heart-warm, sister Rose, new troth-plight and so happy.   *Sits by Rose*

ROSE—Ay, new troth-plight and so happy!

MIRIAM—Nay, will you not look at me? Ay, you must not feel— Indeed, I do not care for John Margeson—no, not one jot. Grieve not for that. For I see, now I have seen other men, how selfish he is, and how cruel— Oh, nay, nay, Rose! Indeed I meant it not! I meant it not!

ROSE—You spoke the truth of him, I think.

MIRIAM—I meant it not. Ah, Rose!

ROSE—You do not love him? You are quite, quite sure you do not love him?

MIRIAM—Oh, quite, quite sure!

ROSE—At least I will be glad for that. That's somewhat. Why, truly yes, Miriam, I am happy. It hath been so merry an evening—so merry! Run you to bed, sweet. I'll make fast the door.

MIRIAM—Come speedily. (*takes candle, goes up stairs*) Good night, Rose!

ROSE—Good night!

    Exit Miriam R3.

A merry evening! A merry—merry evening! (*looks curiously at her wrists*) Nay, there be no cords upon my wrists—yet I can feel them there! And I who promised long ago to kiss the better man! (*takes the letter from floor where it has fallen*) The better man! I shall be John Margeson's wife, as you counselled. I shall be John Margeson's wife—and John will have his right—his right—his— O, mother in Heaven! *Turns sobbing to fireplace.*

> *The door C opens noiselessly, and Garrett drags himself in, bareheaded, coatless, white-faced, in the last stages of exhaustion. He stands leaning against the door-frame, speechless, his eyes upon Rose.*

ROSE—(*with a sense of some one's being in the room, she turns slowly, sees Garrett, and starts forward*) Garrett Foster! Garrett Foster! Here? Here in Plymouth? (*recovers herself; bitterly*) Nay, verily, this is not the way by Monhegan back to England!

GARRETT—Rose!

ROSE—Why have you come?

GARRETT—Faith, what if I came to dance at your wedding, Mistress de la Noye?

ROSE—I have plighted troth to John Margeson this hour—this moment, do you hear?—even as you bade, and because you bade! (*dashes down letter*) I— Garrett! You're spent!   *Starts to him*

GARRETT—No! No, I tell you! No! Don't touch me. I must speak with the Captain. I— Keep your hands from me. 'Sdeath, I can stand straight! *Staggers*

ROSE—(*half supporting him*) Come to the fire! Come!

GARRETT—Not so near yet! I'm chilled enough to freeze the flames.   *Sinks weakly on settle*

Rose—Coatless such a night as this? You have not tramped it down the Massachusetts trail?

Garrett—Nay, I made a trail of mine own through the bushes. I lost my way. Last night I slept in the open. I— Well, 'tis over! 'Tis over! *His head sinks upon his breast.*

Rose—Garrett! Look up! Let me run fetch Captain Standish!

Garrett—Plague o' your Captain! (*catches her skirt*) D'ye think I froze and starved for his sake? I don't want your Captain! I want you, Rose! Rose!

Rose—Garrett! Have pity! Have pity!

Garrett—(*clinging to her, half delirious*) But a moment. I want to look on you. I have thought on you—but this is real. And I'm out o' the snow; 'twas up to my thigh some places, and— God! but the fire is good!

Rose—He's wandering. O, my lad! My poor, poor lad! Let me bring you to drink. (*she gently looses his hold upon her*) Nay, I'll not go out of your sight, Garrett! I'll not go out of your sight! *Crosses to cupboard*

Garrett—It looks as I remembered it. I've thought on this room so many times, there at Wessagusett. There you fight even for the corner you lie in. Always brawling there! Sometimes I could scarce think of you for the brawling.

Rose—(*crosses with a cup*) There! 'Tis the Captain's brandy! Drink!

Garrett—(*drinks, then speaks with the ghost of his old merriment*) It relishes better than the brew you gave me last summer.   Do you remember last summer, little Rose?

ROSE—Remember? I shall remember after I am dead!

GARRETT—Your health! My faith, the same old Rose!

ROSE—No! No, I tell you! I am to marry John Margeson.

GARRETT—Don't speak, O my Rose! Don't speak! Give me this minute. He hath had all the winter; he will have all the days that are to come. Can you not spare me this one minute? Faith, I'm grown humble, even as you could desire! (*rises, draws her into his arms*) Only a minute, only to touch your hand, to look on you—

ROSE—Let me go, Garrett! Let me go! I dare not suffer your lightest touch because—

> *Re-enter John quietly C.*

GARRETT—Because you love him!

ROSE—No! No! Because I hate him. Because I love— No! No! I said naught! I said— (*John closes the door behind him sharply. Rose turns, startled, and sees him. There is an instant's silence. Then she speaks in a breathless voice*) John Margeson!

JOHN—(*coming down*) I am not welcome, then? You have a guest? Ay, as I thought. Good even to you, Garrett Foster!

ROSE—John, listen to me.   Listen!

JOHN—How came you hither?

GARRETT—How else but on my two feet?

JOHN—Howe'er you came, you have broken the edict of banishment.

ROSE—The edict! Garrett!

GARRETT—I have broken also three palings of your rotten stockade. Go mend them. Best take to yourself a hammer and put off your sword, 'less ye can handle it better than last summer.

ROSE—Oh, hush, hush!

JOHN—Let him rail, an he will, lass. When a man's hands are tied, we leave his tongue free.

GARRETT—A pretty similitude, Margeson, but my hands are not tied, nor like to be. Give me to speak with the Captain.

JOHN—Stand, there! Your business is with the Governor.

ROSE—The Governor!

JOHN—What is this gallows' dog to you?

ROSE—He was a good friend to us all. Let him go, John! You head the watch; you have but to leave the way clear. Let him go! Oh, let him go, even as he came! I ask it of you, my first asking, since I gave you the right of my lips.

GARRETT—Right of her lips! Hell burn him!

JOHN—I have a duty to the town, mistress. (*seizes Garrett by the collar*) Come!

ROSE—You coward! He can scarce stand! *Runs to door R.*

JOHN—He need not feign weakness with me. *Flings Garrett off so that he falls to floor.*

Rose —*(calling aloud)* Captain Standish! Captain! Captain!

Re-enter Standish.

Standish—Yes, Rose. What is it? You, Margeson—

Rose—No, no! Look not thither. Only listen to me. Listen! You must be merciful. You have always been. And 'tis because of me he has broken your edict. Promise you will deal gently by him— *Garrett drags himself to his feet. John grasps his arm.*

Standish—Garrett Foster! Here?

Garrett—Let go! *(flings John aside, steps forward unsteadily)* At your service, Captain. The bad penny—

Standish—Silence!

Rose—O, Captain! Captain!

Standish—Peace, Rose! Foster, you bear in mind the words I said to you when I sent you hence. Margeson, conduct this man to the block-house and secure him in close custody.

Rose—Captain! It is not to prison you are sending Garrett Foster—it is to death!

John — His deserts, when he hath had due trial. Come!

Rose—Doth the frost wait till you try a man ere it freezes him? Doth starvation wait, or fever, or mortal pain? I tell you, it is a starving man—a man wasting with fever—a man frozen to the marrow that you are sending to an icy prison—and to his sure death ere it dawn to-morrow! Captain! Captain!

STANDISH—Good God, lass! I tell you, I've no choice. But if food—my cloak—

GARRETT—I'm no beggar—save for one word—alone with you—   *Faint and gasping*

JOHN—He would but stay a moment longer in warmth and fair company. A cunning knave! Come!

STANDISH—'Tis I command here. Stand back! (*to Garrett*) Your word, lad! Be quick!

JOHN—But Captain—

STANDISH—Is this mutiny? (*John salutes and sullenly draws back*) Your word now!

GARRETT—(*with a gasp*) Indians!

STANDISH—(*in angry surprise*) Body of God! *What?*

GARRETT—Don't fright the girl. Indians!

ROSE—I heard and I'm not frighted. Quick—quick! Your news!

GARRETT—The Indians—they're on the warpath! They'll strike here—at Plymouth—in a day—two days at most— *Garrett sinks down on the settle, half unconscious. Rose bends over him.*

JOHN—The man doth but vapor to gain more time. Indians! 'Tis a bugbear dream. Captain, this fellow shall delay no longer.

STANDISH—You say—

JOHN—'Tis not I command. The Governor! (*produces a sealed warrant*) I think you will scarce nay-say this, Captain.   *Hands warrant to Standish*

STANDISH——(*reading*) "Said Garrett Foster—for afore-mentioned seditions—not suffered to pass from juris-diction of colony." You rat! You crawled for this —the instant this lad staggered in, dying, to bring us warning?

JOHN—I know my duty, Captain.

GARRETT—Let be! (*rises unsteadily*) Take me, while yet my feet—

ROSE—Captain! In God's name! You have the power!

STANDISH—I did not know he held the Governor's warrant. My power—I have no power!

JOHN——(*collaring Garrett*) Come!

ROSE—Wait! Wait! Captain! In that warrant you read no word of prison. You said only that he should not pass beyond the jurisdiction of the colony. Don't you see? Don't you see? If you held him here—a prisoner—a paroled prisoner—

STANDISH——(*with a shout of relief*) Well shot, Major Rose! Margeson, take your hands from that man!

JOHN—I'll to the Governor. There's a to-morrow!

ROSE—To-morrow is to-morrow! For to-night Gar-rett Foster rests here, in the guard of the Captain of Plymouth!

STANDISH—Your parole, sir! *With his last strength Garrett draws himself erect, salutes, and falls to floor unconscious. Rose starts to him. John catches her arm and thrusts her back.*

CURTAIN

ACT IV

Scene:—SAME AS ACT III. The shutters are closed so that the room is darkened. Pistols and bags of powder are upon the table. The room is in marked disorder, with chairs overturned or displaced.

At rise of curtain, Barbara has just finished loading a musket at table and is putting it down. Miriam is crouching on the settle, in great terror.

MIRIAM—Oh, what will become of us! What will become of us?

BARBARA—Miriam! Hush you now! Hush!

MIRIAM—(*whimpering*) I'm so frightened! The Indians! Oh, if they get to us!

BARBARA—They will not reach us, not while the Captain guards the town. (*goes to door C, listens*) Listen! You can no longer hear the shots. They have not fired a shot for minutes. The fight is surely over.

MIRIAM—(*sobbing*) Oh! Oh!

BARBARA—And you weep? What wife will you make for a lad with a wilderness to tame, if you flinch at the first note of danger?   *Sets the room to rights*

MIRIAM—Oh, but while the fight was on, down there at the stockade, I was brave—was I not brave? Nay, I did not cry out, not once! I sat quiet here—

BARBARA—And what else should you do, pray? Men cannot be hampered with sobbing women, when they've men's work to do.

MIRIAM—I would be brave, but—oh! oh! the terror of it! Here all was so peaceful—only last night Philippe swore there was no danger—and then—and then this morning, like an awful dream, that sudden flurry of snow and the cry that the savages were upon us—without warning—

BARBARA—Ay, it is not the fashion with savages to send us warning of the hour when they come.

MIRIAM—The cries! The shots! And the room so dark—I know not if it be night or day!

BARBARA—Sure, you would not fling wide the shutters to let in stray arrows?

MIRIAM—(*glancing fearfully at windows*) Oh! Are the shutters fast, think you? Are they fast? Oh, let us bar the door!   *Runs up and bars door*

BARBARA—Bar the door? Then how shall the men run in when they need powder? Come, come! If our Rose were here, she would show you bravery!

MIRIAM—Oh, Rose! Rose! Where is Rose? No doubt she is killed—she and Aunt Resolute! They went forth this morning ere the fight began—I do know in my heart they're killed—

BARBARA—Folly, child! They came safe into the block-house. Did not the men say so?

MIRIAM—Ay, they said so! But I don't believe them! I— (*heavy knocking at door C. Miriam shrieks*) Oh! Oh!

PHILIPPE—(*without*) Open! Open!

MIRIAM—(*falls on her knees*) Oh! Oh! 'Tis the savages!

BARBARA—You silly wench! Do the savages cry in Philippe's voice? 'Tis Philippe!   *Opens door*

   Enter Philippe, in buff jacket, with his musket.

MIRIAM—(*covering her eyes*) O, Philippe! Are you killed? I dare not look! Are you killed?

PHILIPPE—Killed? I killed?

MIRIAM—(*peeping between her fingers*) You are quite sure you're not killed?

PHILIPPE—(*lifts her up and kisses her*) Doth a ghost kiss in this fashion?

BARBARA—And now, if your sweetheart be sufficient comforted, tell us, what news do you bring?

PHILIPPE—Ah, bad news! We have beaten the Indians back and the fight is over. *Throws open shutters. The afternoon sunlight streams in.*

MIRIAM—And you call that bad news, that the fight is over?

PHILIPPE—Why not? I had looked to see a fight in earnest—a grapple, strength to strength—and they never once topped the stockade. A few volleys, and whiff! (*a blown breath*) they were melting back into the forest!

BARBARA—When you have fought as many fights as has the Captain, you will not weep at a fight soon done. How is it with the Captain?

PHILIPPE—Why, hearty and swearing, as in the days when he fought in Flanders! Ay, and he'll have me by the ears, if I hasten not back with the powder.

MIRIAM—Powder! But the fight is over!

PHILIPPE—Ay, but we must keep good guard. And their powder is nearly spent.

BARBARA—(*giving powder*) Run then!

PHILIPPE—I'll run, you may be sure. I'd not have the Captain rate me to-day. *Flings open door C. Aunt Resolute, in a wadded cloak and hood, is seen drooping on the threshold, entirely demoralized.*

PHILIPPE—Why, Mistress Story! Alone?

AUNT RESOLUTE—Don't talk to me! Don't talk to me!

BARBARA—Dear Aunt! 'Tis good to see you safe!

PHILIPPE—Sit ye down, mistress. *Philippe and Barbara help Aunt Resolute to sit by the table. Philippe's musket slips so it points at Aunt Resolute.*

AUNT RESOLUTE—Oh! Don't point that gun at me!

PHILIPPE—(*bewildered*) Gun?

AUNT RESOLUTE—Ay, gun! Gun! Turn it away! Turn it away! (*Philippe shifts musket*) And get you gone, gun and all! You're far too young to be trusted with a gun!

PHILIPPE—(*indignantly*) Mistress Story, there be limits to speech!

BARBARA—There, there! Quickly with that powder!

PHILIPPE—Ay, mistress!

   Exit Philippe C.

AUNT RESOLUTE—The careless jackanapes!

BARBARA—Dear Aunt! To think of you at the block-house, where the fight was sorest!

AUNT RESOLUTE—Ay, well I know it!

BARBARA—Your brave cloak—'tis all besmeared with dirt!

AUNT RESOLUTE—'Tis no wonder. These last hours I have spent a-neighboring with the pumpkins in a snug, dark corner of the cellar. 'Twas a fine dark spot, but not over-salubrious for my rheumatics.

MIRIAM—Oh, the terror of it!

AUNT RESOLUTE—Ay, and rare music did I listen to —whooping of Indians, and bellowing of men, and braying of guns! There sat I, and trembled, and prayed, (*weeps with humiliation*) yea, verily, I have prayed to-day with great fervor! Even I!

BARBARA—Dear Aunt! My heart is sorry for you! There in peril, in the dark, alone—

AUNT RESOLUTE—(*looks up, wickedly*) Alone? Did I say I was alone? Mention it not, niece, lest unseemly stories go abroad in Plymouth, but I was *not* alone!

BARBARA—Not alone? Some other of the women—

AUNT RESOLUTE—Slander not women! 'Twas no woman sought shelter there in the cellar. A fine lusty man— Oh, that such should call themselves men!

BARBARA—A man? A man in hiding, and a good fight toward? The Captain shall deal with him! His name!

AUNT RESOLUTE—Nay, I could not see his face. I but heard his teeth chattering in the dark. (*rises*) But I'll search, and if I find, 'tis one man in Plymouth shall taste the quality of my tongue! Help me hence, lass! (*to Miriam*) It has been a day! *Goes to door R, Miriam helping her.*

BARBARA—Pray you, Aunt!

AUNT RESOLUTE—Eh?

BARBARA—Is our Plymouth still too quiet for your mind?

AUNT RESOLUTE—You'd say—

BARBARA—Does it chance you've found at last, even in our poor little Plymouth, that new sensation for which your soul yearned?

AUNT RESOLUTE—Saucepate!   *Bursts into tears*

> *Exeunt R Aunt Resolute, weeping bitterly, and Miriam.   Barbara begins tying up bags of powder at table.*

> *Enter C Garrett.   He wears a noticeable crimson coat, a little too large for him, and carries a drawn sword in his hand, and a pistol in his belt.*

BARBARA—(*glancing over her shoulder, carelessly*) More comings? Well, what do you here, John Margeson?

GARRETT—If you're talking to John Margeson, mistress, you must speak louder.

BARBARA—Lord save us! You, Garrett Foster? Up on your feet, with a sword in your hand? Why, I thought you were sick, upstairs, in your bed!

GARRETT—Well, I've not died there—to be born again John Margeson. *Comes down and places his sword and pistol on chimney-piece.*

BARBARA—But surely you— What could have called you forth, lad?

GARRETT—Why, I heard a cracking of muskets, and I bethought me of a gap in the stockade—

BARBARA—A gap? In our stockade? Did the Captain—

GARRETT—The Captain knew naught of it. 'Twas a gap I myself made last night to enter, three palings knocked away. So I clapped into what clothes were at hand, and went forth to the gap, and—and when the fight was over, I remembered the parole that I gave not to quit this house.

BARBARA—Ay, your parole! If they saw you, lad!

GARRETT—Nay, I think there's no one knows I have been forth. For we had that gap quite to ourselves—

BARBARA—You say—

GARRETT—Yes, we had it to ourselves—I and an Indian or so!

BARBARA—An Indian?

GARRETT—'Twas not in nature an Indian should not spy that gap. But no Indian came through that gap!

BARBARA—Bless your brave eyes! And to think I could mistake you for John! 'Twas the coat deceived me.

GARRETT—The coat?

BARBARA—Why, sure, 'tis John's old coat you are wearing. There's no mistaking its crimson. 'Twas the talk of the settlement, when that coat was new. How came you by it?

GARRETT—Faith, how do I know? I but know the Captain bade Philippe fetch me a doublet from the spare coats at the Common House—beggar that I am!

BARBARA—Nay, hush, lad! I remember. And he brought thee this?

GARRETT—'Twas by my bed when I woke. And so 'twas Margeson's coat? Lie you there! *Strips off coat*

and flings it down by stairway, where it lies almost con-
cealed.   It is now seen that his right forearm is bandaged
with a blood-soaked handkerchief.

BARBARA—Save us!   Your arm is hurt!

GARRETT—Ay.   An arrow.   I had to cut it out.
And this rag is untidily soaked.   Good mistress, can
you find me a fresh bandage?

BARBARA—Ay.   I'll run for an old linen—

GARRETT—Spare trouble!   *(starts to stairs)*   I'll tear a
strip from one of the sheets.

BARBARA—From my sheets?   From my well-beloved
English sheets?   Now do sheets grow on bushes at
Wessagusett?   *(fetches old napkin from cupboard and*
bandages his arm)   An you tear my sheets, you'll find
you'll need do more than guard us from the savages
ere I forgive you.

GARRETT—I'll remember.   And I thank you, mis-
tress.   *Kisses her hand*

BARBARA—There!   Get you to your bed, lest they
guess you broke parole.

    Exit Garrett up stairs and to chamber R3.

A brave lad!   Oh, my poor little Rose!

PHILIPPE—*(without)* Come!   Come you in!

ROSE—*(without)* No!   No!   I don't wish to come
in!   I—

    Enter C Philippe, holding Rose by the wrist.   Her
    hair is disordered, her cap held in place by a single
    pin, her kerchief rumpled, her cloak slipping from her

shoulder. She carries a powder-horn slung over her shoulder, and her face and hands are smudged with black powder stains.

PHILIPPE—Now shame upon you! You, a lass! Loading of guns at the stockade, there among the men, as if you were a boy!

ROSE—(*gaily*) Oh, la, la, little brother! You were vastly glad an hour agone, when 'twas your gun I loaded!

PHILIPPE—And you, a girl! You would not find Miriam Chillingsley doing such deeds.

ROSE—Now since when am I to pattern myself by Miriam Chillingsley? Miriam load a gun? Oh, la! Miriam would load a gun from the big end of the powder-horn—so! I tell you, she would, Philippe, she would, she would!

BARBARA—Philippe! Why, what is this clamor?

PHILIPPE—Where think you that I found her, this madcap sister of mine? There at the stockade, there where the firing was hottest—all black with powder, loading the guns—

ROSE—Ay, and the Governor—the Governor, mark you!—he saw me there, too, and what think you he said?

BARBARA—That you were best bide elsewhere, since you broke from the rule of the Captain's wife.

ROSE—Nay, he said he was proud that Plymouth owned so good and brave a soldier! The honor of it! Straightway I felt myself grow taller by an inch or twain. Do you not mark it?   *Stands on tiptoe*

BARBARA—Dear heart! Ah, my Rose, 'tis good to hear you speak in the old tone, 'tis good to hear you laugh!

ROSE—Laugh? What else should I do? Last night I wept and wept, until I think I can never weep again. Done is done, Mistress Standish, done is done. And 'tis a sweet spring day, and we have fought a brave fight, and I tell you, the music of the guns can drown the cry of a heartache!

BARBARA—Brave little lass!

ROSE—Ay, done is done! And I—I am to marry a worthy man who—can care for me. Nay, no more tears! (*turns to Philippe*) Why, who's sulking here? You know what's gone amiss with Philippe? He's jealous!

PHILIPPE—(*angrily*) Rose!

ROSE—Ay, he's jealous that the Governor called me a brave soldier while he—he— You know what the Governor bade him do?

PHILIPPE—You minx!

ROSE—The Governor bade him come back here to the house and guard the women. Poor Philippe!

BARBARA—And are we not worth guarding?

PHILIPPE—No! Not while the other men strengthen the stockade and do man's work. Well, 'tis John Margeson I can thank that I am put to this service. He's done it to spite me, because of the matter of his coat.

ROSE—What of his coat?

PHILIPPE—Why, I fetched some clothes for Garrett from the Common House, and John says 'twas his coat I took.   A churlish fellow to begrudge a coat to Garrett Foster who saved the settlement!

ROSE—Ay, Garrett's warning saved the settlement. They all know it.   They all say it.   'Twas Garrett. Mistress Standish, how is he now?

BARBARA—Sleeping soundly, I pray.

PHILIPPE—Sleeping?   Through all this turmoil?   Verily, he hath learned to be an arrant sleepyhead at Wessagusett!

BARBARA—Ah, let him rest, poor lad!   He hath well earned it.   I think there is somewhat of fever upon him.   Let him rest.

ROSE—(*coming to Philippe, earnestly*) Philippe!   You are not angry with me in earnest?   Look at me, little brother!   No, don't look like that!   Ah, Philippe, be gentle with me!   Indeed, indeed, my heart is sore! And you—you are all is left me.

PHILIPPE—Rose!   I meant it not!   There, there, dear!

ROSE—Not a very merry way to crave your countenance, is it?   But I'll be merry straightway, and we'll be good comrades, as we used, won't we, Philippe?
    Starts to pat his cheek with a powder-blackened hand

PHILIPPE—Ay, surely!   *Catches her wrist, looks disapprovingly at her hand.*

ROSE—(*laughing*) It is black, *n'est-ce pas?*   Well, I'll run within and wash my black away.   But I'll return speedily, Philippe, speedily!

Exit Rose R.

PHILIPPE—Dear lass! Ah, Mistress Standish, to see her there at the stockade, where any moment a chance arrow— Ah, if Miriam had gone with her! I—I— Perchance, now the fight is over, Miriam would venture forth again now?

BARBARA—Are you there at last? Nay, I'll tell her as I go one stays for her without.

Exit Barbara R.

PHILIPPE—I thank you, mistress.

Re-enter Miriam R.

MIRIAM—O, Philippe! (*hides her face on his breast*) Oh, I was so frightened!

PHILIPPE—There, there, sweetheart! You're not frightened now. Come, sit you down. We have a grave matter to speak on. *Philippe and Miriam sit on settle.*

MIRIAM—A grave matter? (*alarmed*) Oh, surely, the Indians are not come to attack us again?

PHILIPPE—The Indians are gone. Put the Indians from your mind. 'Tis graver far than that. Miriam, how shall we go about to tell Rose?

MIRIAM—Tell Rose?

PHILIPPE—Why, that we have plighted troth.

MIRIAM—Oh, but she will not be angry. She hath a plighted lover of her own. So you have but to tell her gently—

PHILIPPE—I tell her? I?

Miriam—Why, surely!

Philippe—Now I—I should hold it a woman's place. And two lassies together know sweet ways to tell secrets. 'Twould be very seemly if you—

Miriam—Nay, that I'll not! And fie upon you for a coward to ask it of me!

Philippe—Did you ever see my sister in her anger?

Miriam—Nay, to me she is ever gentle.

Philippe—I *have* seen her.

Miriam—But surely so young a maid—so small—

Philippe—The maid may be small, but not so is the anger. Ah, 'tis a grave matter indeed! How shall I tell her? How—

Miriam—Whate'er you say, you must be very gentle.

Philippe—I have it! Look you, I'll say somewhat of Margeson and her betrothal—

Miriam—Excellent! She will say how happy she is, and then you will say—

Philippe—Then I'll say that no doubt she will wish to see me happy too. Why, 'tis an easy task!

Miriam—Yes, yes!

Rose—(*within*) Philippe!

Miriam—Good lack, she's coming!

Philippe—Nay, perhaps after all, 'twere better that you—that you—

Miriam—That I'll not! 'Tis you shall tell her! 'Tis you, I say! *Runs up to window*

Re-enter Rose, tidy and without her cloak, with knitting in her hand.

ROSE—Ah, Philippe! I'll wager you know not what I am knitting here.   *Sits by table*

PHILIPPE—(*going to her*) Knitting? It looked to me as if you did but snarl the yarn. Now, when Miriam knits—

ROSE—Oh, I care not to hear of Miriam! What is it I am knitting, tell me!

PHILIPPE—I—I—

ROSE—Oh, little brother, you are dull to-day! I am knitting you a pair of stockings. I've neglected you shamefully these last months.

PHILIPPE—And am I to wait for stockings till you have knit these?

ROSE—(*counting stitches laboriously*) One, two! Ay.

PHILIPPE—Verily, I am glad that summer is coming.

ROSE—Jackanapes!

MIRIAM—(*aside to Philippe*) Tell her now, now while she is merry.

ROSE—You shall see how fast I can knit. The stockings will be ready before the winter.

PHILIPPE—Yes, I see.

MIRIAM—Tell her! *Crosses to fireplace. After a moment takes down Garrett's pistol from chimney-piece and very gingerly handles it.*

PHILIPPE—Rose—er—er—I saw John Margeson this morning.

Rose—(*soberly*) Yes. You told me.

Philippe—I have hardly had chance to say that I—I wish you happy in your betrothal to him.

Rose—(*sadly, touching his hand*) I thank you.

Philippe—(*looking helplessly at Miriam*) But—but— you see— (*to Rose*) Surely you are happy in your betrothal, sister?

Rose—Oh, don't speak of this to me—not yet, little brother, not yet, dear!

Philippe—Sister!   *Sits on table near her*

Rose—I don't want to think of John Margeson—not this one good hour.   I don't want to think of last night.   I want to believe I am back with you in the old days, good comrades as we used to be.   Philippe, do you remember, when you would wheedle something from me, how you used to coax me and call me Sweetheart Rose?   Call me that now, as we used!

Philippe—Ay, as we used, dear Rose!

Rose—Say "Sweetheart Rose"!

Philippe—(*rising*) Nay, sister, 'tis foolish, but I did promise her who is my sweetheart indeed that I would never say sweetheart to—

Rose—Your sweetheart indeed!

Miriam—(*hurts her hand with pistol*) Oh!

Philippe—(*crosses, takes pistol from Miriam*)   Take heed how you play with that pistol!   If you were hurt, sweetheart!   *Kisses her*

ROSE—(*springing up*) Oh! Philippe de la Noye! How dare you!

MIRIAM—Is this your gentle telling? You've spoilt all! Let me go! Let me go!

PHILIPPE—Oh, but a stockade fight is sport to this! Now if you plight troth to a man, why may not I to a maid?

ROSE—Plighted troth? Miriam, you should take shame to yourself. My only brother—all I have in the world— I did but lend him to you and you've stolen him from me—you've—

PHILIPPE—Peace, I say, Rose! Will you make her weep?

ROSE—Ay, she must not shed a tear, your sweetheart, and you care not though I cry my eyes blind.

MIRIAM—Oh, Rose, prithee—prithee—

ROSE—Don't touch me! My only brother! All— all I had!

MIRIAM—O, cruel! Would you alone be happy?

ROSE—I—happy? Nay, I would alone be—unhappy. What right have I— O, Miriam, forgive me! I was selfish. I was cruel. Forgive me, little sister. *Takes Miriam in her arms.*

PHILIPPE—The Lord fought for me!

ROSE—There, go now—go! 'Tis a strange day—a strange day! Philippe, take your—sweetheart, and God go with you!   *Philippe kisses Rose's hand*

   Exeunt Philippe R, with Miriam.

Even Philippe! Even my brother! Oh, I'm alone—alone!

Re-enter on stairs Garrett, coatless, in a clean shirt, the sleeve of which covers the bandage on his arm.

ROSE—Oh! You have risen?

GARRETT—At last! (*comes down stairs*) I take shame to myself for a laggard.

ROSE—Ay, well you may! For while you slept, a good fight has been fought. Oh, no, no, Garrett! I know not what I say! You were spent, you were ill. 'Twas well that you could sleep.

GARRETT—Ay, 'twas well. For I had a good dream.

ROSE—A dream?

GARRETT—I dreamed that all that happened here last night was a dream—all but one moment.

ROSE—One moment?

GARRETT—(*passionately*) The moment when—

ROSE—The moment that you must forget.

GARRETT—Rose!

ROSE—Ah, not like that, Garrett! You must never speak to me like that—never again! The night is over, we are sane now, in the daylight, are we not? And—and I am a plighted wife.

GARRETT—(*bitterly*) Ay, plighted to a—

ROSE—Hush! He is to be my husband.

GARRETT—Rose! (*catches her hand*) Forgive me! I was a brute to lay more upon you. I—

ROSE—I pray you, let go my hand.

GARRETT—Sure, you can suffer that much—just the touch of a friend's hand? You've not cast me out utterly from your—friendship? Nay, I'll speak of naught that may offend you, I swear it. Only to touch your hand—there is no wrong in that? Nor in that we speak together for one little moment. 'Tis for the last time.

ROSE—Garrett!   *Sits on settle*

GARRETT—Ay, an they set me free, I shall get me back to England.

ROSE—Yes! Back to England! And then?

GARRETT—Then to the wars!

ROSE—Yes.

GARRETT—When I am gone, I wonder—will you ever think upon me, Rose?

ROSE—I shall not forget you. I do not forget my—friends. When I sit at my wheel, in—my husband's house, I shall think on you, and I shall pray God that you speed well—indeed, I shall pray it! I shall pray it!   *Rises, turns away*

GARRETT—I shall speed the better in that your prayers go with me. I—Rose!   *Catches her to him*

ROSE—Oh, no! No! It is the end—it is the end! I cannot make you a mere friend, not even to give myself these moments with you, with an honest heart I cannot! We must not speak—we must not see each other, never again. Oh, my dear, can't you see?

I'm afraid of you! I'm afraid of myself! *Turns away, hiding her face.*

GARRETT—Forgive me this that I have wrung from you. 'Tis for the last time.   *Goes toward stairs*

    Enter John C.

JOHN—Good morrow to you, Rose. *Stands at foot of stairs.*

GARRETT—Let me pass hence.

JOHN—'Tis a high tone you take for a jail-bird.

GARRETT—But you are not my jailer. You! Will you tell me now that the Indians were my bugbear dream? Next time, believe my warnings.

JOHN—You came to warn the settlement! You came to Plymouth to steal my holdings—and you came an hour too late!

ROSE—Oh!

JOHN—You can make your boast of saving the settlement—you always were a braggart! But the girl is mine—you hear me? Now you may go hence. (*comes down*) The Governor hath set you free.

ROSE—(*joyfully*) Free?

JOHN—Ay, free! He hath given you back your parole for this brave deed of yours—and you are free. Free to go to the devil, an you will! (*turns to Rose*) Rose, my sweetheart! Where is my kiss? *Starts to kiss her*

ROSE—(*shrinking*) John! No, no!

GARRETT—(*under his breath*) God!   *Opens door C*

ROSE—Garrett!   *Runs to him as if for protection*

JOHN—By what right, mistress, do you hold him here?

ROSE—What right? (*wildly*) That he is a sick man, a fevered man—

GARRETT—Nay, let me go! There is less fever upon me alone, out under the sky!

>   *Exit Garrett C.*

ROSE—Garrett! O, Garrett! *Leans against door, with face hidden.*

JOHN—Truly, 'tis a lover-like greeting you give me, mistress.

ROSE—(*turns to him*) John! I—I have to speak with you. You will listen? Oh, you will listen?

JOHN—(*curtly*) I'll listen.

ROSE—You know—you know I said last night—I said that I would marry you—

JOHN—Ay, I have your promise. And you said once you kept your promises.

ROSE—Ay, and I'll stand to what I said, unless— unless— But for your own sake— Ah, John Margeson, you know, you know! I was mad last night, mad when I pledged myself to you. I never loved you. I could not love you. You know the man I love.

JOHN—I know that once, here in this very spot, you taunted me with breach of faith, because of a gossips' rumor. You're not so strict to-day in the matter of keeping faith. Remember, mistress, whate'er was said of me, I never broke my solemn word.

ROSE—Nor have I. Nor will I. You have my pledge, you will do with me as you list. But my heart—

look in my eyes, John Margeson!—never will you have my heart—never—to eternity!

JOHN—Let your heart stray, if it dare, so that I have you— (*catches her in his arms*) you—the you I hold —that I hold from Garrett Foster.

ROSE—Oh! Oh!   *A long shudder*

JOHN—I have your pledge, I say—your solemn pledge that you may not break, not till the day I, too, prove a false speaker.

Enter Standish C in armor, with his musket.

STANDISH—Margeson!   Well met!

JOHN—(*apprehensively*) What would you, Captain?

STANDISH—Nay, lad, I want but to look upon you, for verily you stand a new man in my eyes!

JOHN—(*starts and shrinks*) Captain, what—

STANDISH—John, this many a day I've wronged you in my thoughts.   Rose, your woman's eyes saw clearer than my own to this man's heart.

ROSE—John, what does he mean?

JOHN—Nay, I—I—

STANDISH—I mean, lass, 'tis thanks to this man, your plighted lover, that the settlement this day was saved from the savages.

Re-enter Garrett C, and Philippe R, and listen intently.

ROSE—What!   Captain!

STANDISH—There was a breach in the stockade, and John Margeson held that breach alone until we brought him help.   Then he slipped away.   The snow was so thick, faith, John, I could not have guessed who fought that fight, but for the crimson of that old coat of thine that gleamed through the snow.

JOHN—My crimson coat!   God!

GARRETT—(*starting forward*) Captain!

ROSE—And John—John's fight saved the settlement! Oh, I can bear life the better!

PHILIPPE—(*in amazement*) His fight saved the settlement?   It was John Margeson who held the stockade?

STANDISH—John Margeson and no other.   (*to Garrett*) Foster, you would speak with me?

GARRETT—I—I—(*hesitates, looking at Rose*) Oh, 'twas naught.   They say you sail this night with aid to Wessagusett.   Let me go with you, Captain!   Let me go with you!

STANDISH—Have your will.   Get your arms!   John, bid them beat the long roll in the street.   Philippe, look to my musket, (*tosses it to Philippe*) then bear it to the shallop.   We sail within the hour.

> *Exeunt Standish C, Philippe R.   John starts to door C, but pauses by window in thought.   Rose starts to door R.   Garrett goes to her.*

GARRETT—Rose!   You are happier for that John Margeson bore himself bravely to-day?

ROSE—Must I not be happier?   He may be harsh and bitter, but he is a brave man.   I can at least respect him.   Oh, it is far, far easier now—this troth-plight that I cannot break.

GARRETT—I would make all things easier for you, God knows! *Impulsively Rose catches his hand in hers, laying her left hand on his arm. She touches the wound and involuntarily he shrinks with pain.*

ROSE—Garrett! Your arm! You're wounded!

GARRETT—Nothing! A scratch—an old hurt that opened last night. And you believe that I would make you happy, were it in my power?

ROSE—I believe it, Garrett.

    Exit Rose R.

GARRETT—God keep you happy! *Takes a pistol and a cleaning rag from table, turns to door C.*

JOHN—(*coming forward*) Garrett Foster!

GARRETT—Ay?

JOHN—Touching that coat—

GARRETT—Your crimson coat—the coat that man wore who fought at the broken stockade?

JOHN—Ay. Do you— Will you—

GARRETT—(*looking him in the face*) I will not make it known—no, never!—what man wore that coat.

JOHN—(*holding out his hand*) Foster, I—

GARRETT—(*striking down his hand savagely*) Damn you! Is it for your sake I keep that silence?

    Re-enter Rose and Philippe R. John goes slowly out C. Garrett steps through door and stands watching him go.

PHILIPPE—Rose, dear! We did not know him.

You've chosen wisely.   What!   There are tears in your eyes!

ROSE—No, no, I say!   I will not weep—not yet! 'Twas just when they two stood here together— Nay, John is a brave man.   Oh, I must not look back.   I must not look back!   *Philippe kisses her*

> *Exit Philippe C.   Garrett presently re-enters and stands by window, cleaning his pistol awkwardly with his left hand, his back to the room.*

ROSE—And yet life goes on with me.   There will be going up and down, and daily tasks to do, ay, and to seem merry in the face of the world.   Merry!   I wonder if I shall ever laugh again.   Well, at least I can set the room to rights, like a good housewife—a fit wife for John Margeson!   (*sets room to rights, spies the crimson coat on the floor*)   What is that?   Why, what is here? (*picks up coat*)   Whose coat?   Oh, John's coat—the crimson coat the Captain knew him by.   How comes it here?   (*looks at Garrett, who is back to her, then at coat*)   If it were—O, God!   If it were!   (*hides coat behind her*)   Garrett!   (*imperatively*)   Garrett!

GARRETT—Ay.   Did you call, Rose?   *Comes down, still cleaning pistol.*

ROSE—What do you there?   How awkwardly you work!   Is it your old wound makes your arm so slow, so clumsy—your *old* wound?

GARRETT—(*sadly*)   Old wounds are slow to heal.
            Rose presses her hand on the hurt place; he shrinks

ROSE—And that old wound—it seems strangely tender

—for an old wound! Had I not best look to it, ere you go?

GARRETT—I tell you, it is nothing. Nay, do not touch me!

ROSE—How was it you said you were hurt?

GARRETT—A knife cut.

ROSE—A knife cut? (*with feigned carelessness*) Then 'twas you yourself did cut the arrow from your wound?

GARRETT—(*falling into her trap*) Surely! Who else was there to cut it out?

ROSE—Then it was an arrow! It was an arrow—no old wound—an arrow—shot to-day—cut out to-day—

GARRETT—Nay, what are you saying? I—

ROSE—Peace, I say! Look at this coat—this crimson coat—look, look! Here in the sleeve, an arrow-cut—an arrow-cut!

GARRETT—Rose!

ROSE—Here in the sleeve, above the place where you bear a bandaged arm. Hath John Margeson a wound, old or new? Did John Margeson wear that coat to-day? Did John Margeson fight that fight to-day? Nay, 'twas you—and you would have given him that fight for my happiness' sake!

Re-enter Standish and John C.

STANDISH—Rose! What outcry is this?

ROSE—A cry that shall ring through Plymouth! 'Twas Garrett Foster, not John Margeson, that fought that fight to-day—it was Garrett Foster, not John Margeson, that saved the settlement!

JOHN—(*coming down to Garrett*) Curse you! You told it—you told it! You told 'twas you wore my coat!

ROSE—He did not tell it! 'Tis you who tell it—you! Captain, you heard—you heard!

STANDISH—(*sternly*) I heard what he must answer to!

JOHN—(*to Rose, piteously*) You would betray me—you who plighted troth—who promised—

ROSE—Whose promise was to be mine again—you said it!—when I proved you spoke false. Have you spoke false here, when you claimed this man's good fight—a coward's lie—yes or no—yes or no? (*John turns away in silence*) Ah!

STANDISH—(*motions to door C, with the same gesture he used to Garrett in Act I*) Go out before me! *John goes out C, with head bent.*

GARRETT—(*incredulously*) Rose!

STANDISH—Rose! You will break faith—

ROSE—Nay, Captain, by your leave, I will keep faith —the faith I pledged long ago, when I swore to kiss the better man!   *Holds out her hands to Garrett*

CURTAIN

Addenda

The borders and cover design of this book were drawn by S. L. Busha. The portrait used on the cover, and the frontispiece are from photographs by Schloss; plates facing pages 30 and 84 are from Byron photographs; and the plate facing page 56 is from a photograph by Fredericks.

CPSIA information can be obtained
at www.ICGtesting.com
Printed in the USA
LVHW102254120821
695208LV00013B/615

9 781148 227474